PLACE IN RETURN BOX to remove this checkout from your record.
TO AVOID FINES return on or before date due.

DATE DUE	DATE DUE	DATE DUE
FEB 2 3 8 97	APR 0 7 2012	
	1 0 2 8 11	
SEP 0 3 1999		
il: 2574204		

MSU Is An Affirmative Action/Equal Opportunity Institution
c:\circ\datedue.pm3-p.1

MEASURING THE IMPACT OF INFORMATION ON DEVELOPMENT

MEASURING THE IMPACT OF INFORMATION ON DEVELOPMENT

Editor:
Michel J. Menou

INTERNATIONAL DEVELOPMENT RESEARCH CENTRE
Ottawa • Cairo • Dakar • Johannesburg • Montevideo • Nairobi
New Delhi • Singapore

Published by the International Development Research Centre
PO Box 8500, Ottawa, ON, Canada K1G 3H9

© International Development Research Centre 1993

Menou, M.J.

Measuring the impact of information on development. Ottawa, ON,
IDRC, 1993. xiii + 188 p.: ill.

/Information/, /economic and social development/, /benefit analysis/,
/project evaluation/, /evaluation techniques/, /indicators/ — /computer
conferencing/, /cost–benefit analysis/, /models/, /input–output/,
/conference reports/, /case studies/, references.

UDC: 007:338   ISBN 0-88936-708-6

A microfiche edition is available.

Contents

———■———

Foreword vii

Preface ix

Acknowledgments xiii

Chapter 1
The Computer Conference 1

Chapter 2
Background Considerations 15

Chapter 3
Benefits 37

Chapter 4
Indicators and Assessment Methods 63

Chapter 5
The Post-Conference Workshop 81

Chapter 6
Preliminary Framework for Impact Assessment 89

Chapter 7
Suggestions for Future Activities 105

Appendices

1. List of Participants 115
2. Applying CBA to an Information Project 121
3. A Rural Community Resource Centre 120
4. Criteria of the US Government Accounting Office 135
5. Applying the Assessment Framework 141

Acronyms and Abbreviations 161

Bibliography 163

Index 183

FOREWORD

———■———

We read increasingly about our entry into the "information age" and the consequent implications for our day-to-day lives. We are becoming accustomed to such terms as "information revolution," "information economy," and "information society." Even if adequate definitions are sometimes elusive, these terms convey a sense of the profound transformation being fueled by changes in the management, role, value, and use of information. But do we fully recognize and understand this transformation? How widespread is the phenomenon? More specifically, to what extent do developing countries participate in and benefit from these changes? In short, what is the impact of information on development?

This issue has intrigued me for some time. Working in the international information field for many years, I have seen numerous projects that have helped improve information systems and services in developing countries, built human and institutional capacity to manage and exploit the information resource, and resulted in information being used to solve specific problems of development. However, evaluation of these interventions has usually been related to short-term outputs. A number of larger questions remain unanswered. Are people convinced of the long-term relevance of the services being offered? Do policymakers have enough evidence to persuade them that allocating resources to the information infrastructure is a wise investment? Can development assistance agencies see the benefits and viability of the information activities they have been called upon to support?

Answering such questions is a complex challenge requiring an intensive multidisciplinary, long-term approach, which is beyond the reach of an individual researcher or institution. This is why our understanding of the impact of information on development has remained largely anecdotal. This report documents a recent initiative that, through its methods and focus, aims to provide a realistic starting point. It surveys the terrain to be covered, identifies the destination, and offers a route map for reaching it. Michel Menou has done a masterful job of weaving together the input of dozens of information users and providers, policymakers, information scientists, and others from the South and the North.

However, even this work is little more than a beginning. The assessment framework that evolved in the course of this study still requires extensive field-testing. This next phase is just starting in a modest way at the International Development Research Centre, but it holds much potential for a concerted program of international collaboration. I hope that this book will serve as a catalyst for such a cooperative effort, one that will ultimately confirm the impact of information on development.

Martha B. Stone
Director General
Information Sciences and Systems Division
International Development Research Centre

PREFACE

———■———

The problem

For several decades, institutions in developing countries and development assistance agencies have supported the evolution of information infrastructures in developing countries. This encompassed the establishment or strengthening of information services at all levels — corporate, local, national, regional, and international — as well as facilitating access to the world's information resources, education and training of information specialists and users, and elaboration of information policies and plans.

Although we have witnessed a steady growth in the provision of information services in developing countries, a number of fundamental questions remain unanswered. The people of these countries question the relevance and appropriateness of the services offered. Development assistance agencies are concerned about problems of sustainability. The extent to which information services actually contribute to the empowerment of people and the accountability of the institutions concerned are subjects of controversy and concern. Logic dictates that information is an essential resource for the social and economic development of Third World countries, but how can this be demonstrated? Information can be a powerful catalyst to transform society, but how tangible is the linkage between information investments and the achievement of specific development goals? The limited status accorded to information in most developing countries suggests that its potential value is not self-evident.

The assessment of development efforts in information infrastructure and services has mainly relied upon measures of input or immediate output. Although information specialists point to internal developments and claim, for example, that a 5 000-record database is now operational, policymakers and decision-makers understandably look for a clear indication of its overall socioeconomic benefits, and ask "so what?"

The answer, so far, has been axiomatic. It is expressed in sentences such as "Information is the most critical resource and plays a fundamental role in development." Yet, there is no systematic body of empirical evidence to support this assertion, especially quantitative evidence (Saracevic 1980). Unless a more appropriate answer is found, people involved in information-related programs will have difficulty justifying a high level of priority and a share of scarce resources compared with those in disciplines whose relation to development is better established.

The challenge for the information science community is to identify meaningful parameters or indicators, qualitative or quantitative, by which the overall socioeconomic impact of information programs and services can be assessed and procedures to allow the gathering of relevant data. The parameters or indicators must be able to provide concrete answers to those who control the allocation of resources at any level in the process of policy formulation and decision-making.

In this context, it is not appropriate to restrict information activities to those in any particular institution, such as libraries or documentation centres (King et al. 1976; Borko and Menou 1983). Rather, one must consider all roles and functions in the communication cycle, from information generation to use, and not exclude any medium, process, or organizational arrangement.

The project

This project was designed as the first phase in a longer term effort to explore the abovementioned problem. It encompassed a computer conference and a post-conference workshop.

The computer conference was the first step. It was exploratory in nature, and its aim was to attempt a thorough and systematic analysis of the benefits likely to be associated with investments in the information infrastructure and information activities in general, then to identify meaningful indicators (qualitative and quantitative) by which those benefits and their impact could be measured.

In a second stage, the outcome of the computer conference was reviewed at a workshop attended by a limited number of the participants from the computer conference and several policymakers and practitioners, mostly from developing countries. They examined the validity and applicability of the theoretical models and assessment methods contained in the summary report of the computer conference and formulated a comprehensive framework for field-testing the results in developing countries.

The output of this project is a conceptual framework and methods, although still preliminary, on the basis of which a number of action-research projects will be undertaken to validate the selected approaches for assessing the impact of information on development and to gather related evidence. This will constitute the next phase of research.

We hope that the momentum provided by this project will result in a number of research activities and field experiments within the information science community and elsewhere directed toward the investigation of these issues. We also hope that a suitable mechanism will be put in place to ensure the monitoring, evaluation, and consolidation of activities occurring during subsequent phases, as well as of their methods and results, so that a substantive body of knowledge will emerge.

The International Development Research Centre (IDRC) and the project's participants are fully aware that this project and, more specifically, the computer conference represent pioneer endeavours and have associated risks and challenges. To the best of our knowledge, this is the first time in the information science community that an international research computer conference has been organized, a thorough examination of the role of information in development and its assessment undertaken, and a structured collective effort toward such an investigation been attempted.

In compiling and editing the report of the computer conference, care was taken to provide a fair and comprehensive account of the discussions and to reflect the contribution of all those involved. Additions were limited to what seemed necessary to clarify particular points. A number of issues may have called for further discussion or comments beyond the conference, but these were deliberately avoided, as much as possible, to keep from distorting the outcome of the exchanges within the conference. Similarly, the section on the post-conference workshop is primarily based upon the reports of its two working groups and notes from the plenary session during which their findings were summarized.

The future directions outlined in this book (Chapters 6 and 7) originally reflected the personal views of the moderator of the computer conference. They were revised during discussion of the draft report by the participants and later incorporated to a large extent in the conclusions of the post-conference workshop. They further include a consolidated and integrated framework for impact assessment that, although it relies mainly upon the submissions of both working groups, was not discussed under this form. It may be considered as one of the main outputs of the project. Furthermore, this section incorporates a summary of related activities initiated by IDRC after the computer conference and workshop.

The documents resulting from the computer conference and post-conference workshop (see Bibliography) will be made available by IDRC, upon request, to concerned researchers and practitioners wishing to undertake further investigation of the subject.

Michel J. Menou

ACKNOWLEDGMENTS

———■———

The participants in the project reported here are grateful to the International Development Research Centre and especially Martha B. Stone, Director General of its Information Sciences and Systems Division, for undertaking this activity and providing effective support for its successful implementation. J.B. Black and D. Balson also deserve special thanks for their guidance and assistance with regard to telecommunications and the use of the computer conferencing system. I also wish to thank D. Ryerson for her skilfull and patient work with the manuscript and P. McConnell for his ongoing input and support as the manager of the project.

The editor is deeply indebted to those who have been involved, in one form or another, in the two parts of the project for their invaluable input to the discussions and support in the implementation of this challenging endeavour.

Chapter 1

THE COMPUTER CONFERENCE

———————■———————

Objectives

The computer conference was expected to permit the identification of

- Significant short- and long-term benefits resulting from the various kinds of information activities;

- Meaningful parameters, or indicators, both qualitative and quantitative, by which these benefits could be assessed;

- Procedures that would allow the gathering of relevant raw data; and

- When appropriate, the methods by which the suggested indicators could be calculated.

In other words, what is the contribution of information activities to development and how can it be assessed? However, the conference was not intended to provide a complete or final answer to the many problems raised by this question. This can only result from empirical studies in the field. A basic framework is required for undertaking such studies and the project's goal was to develop an initial blueprint suitable for undertaking impact assessments in the future. The computer conference had to encompass a broad perspective from its inception, while maintaining a focus on its primary objective.

Meaningful answers to the above question are long overdue

requisites for a more appropriate design of information systems and services that would increase their use, their relevance to both development and the organizations in which they operate, and their sustainability. Such answers may also provide a better understanding of the "information society" and "knowledge society." The problem is of immediate concern to those who need a rationale for their decisions regarding the support and management of information activities, whether they belong to the public, private, or not-for-profit sector of the developing countries or the donor countries; this is especially important to development agencies (Stone 1992). The subject is relevant to all societies; however, the focus of the conference was on developing countries.

Although a number of theoretical and conceptual issues were expected to arise during the conference, its goal was to produce results that could readily be applied. It focused on benefits and related parameters or indicators that could readily be measured and on concrete assessment. Special attention was to be given to indicators that were likely to produce the required evidence of socio-economic benefits, and possibly returns, as a basis for making decisions about investment in information activities.

The resulting framework may be used in retrospective evaluations or decisions regarding ongoing information activities. However, it was primarily meant to offer guidance in the design of future field studies and action research for the evaluation of information services and programs. We believed that the computer conference might also suggest new forms of information-related projects, or components to be included in traditional ones, to enable such assessments, as well as items to be part of an agenda for future research on the relation between information and development.

The computer conference was not expected to produce actual evaluations or measures, nor an appraisal of current information-related programs. However, possible limitations of the latter with regard to their ability to yield the identified benefits or to permit their assessment could be highlighted.

Why a computer conference?

The complexity and difficulty of this subject are conspicuous. Not only has little empirical research been attempted in this area, but there is no commonly agreed upon model to guide the investigation. Therefore, we believed that an uninhibited and in-depth discussion over a long enough time was necessary.

Conventional methods would have required much time spent in preparing and reviewing papers and synthesizing collective summaries. At least two meetings would have been necessary. This approach would not have allowed for the level and duration of interaction that the scope and purpose of the conference required. In view of the time constraints and geographic location of those likely to contribute, a computer conference appeared to be the more appropriate mechanism, in spite of the fact that it excluded a number of potential participants based in parts of the world where telecommunication facilities are inadequate.

Based on previous experience, IDRC selected the CoSy computer conferencing system at the University of Guelph, Canada, as the facility for holding the conference. Although it was recognized that the use of a technology that was unfamiliar to a number of participants might result in some inhibition, we thought this conferencing technique would offer a better opportunity to follow Robert Jungk's (1969) advice that such an effort should be

> Devoted to speculative thinking about the subjects under discussion and at such "crystal-ball" sessions the old style of presenting findings together with the corresponding evidence will be replaced by a spirit of bold speculation, of free-ranging intellectual experimenting and of relaxed give and take. An atmosphere of gaiety and of joint search might then replace the atmosphere of so many gatherings today, marked as it is by self-assertiveness, aggressiveness and possessive pride.

Participants

In view of the complexity of the subject as well as the objective of producing concrete results within a relatively short time, participation was restricted to a limited number of specialists with a recognized expertise in the subject. The number of regular participants was also chosen to allow for the most effective interaction within the group and a joint commitment toward the achievement of the conference objectives.

The conference theme required a multidisciplinary approach. The usefulness of including specialists from a number of disciplines and backgrounds outside the information science community was fully acknowledged. However, such inclusion at this stage was considered inappropriate, because of the inconsistencies in experiences, reference frameworks, concepts, and vocabulary it was likely to introduce. This interaction was foreseen at later stages.

A core group of 16 specialists from the private, government, and academic sectors in North America, Europe, the Caribbean, Latin America, and the Middle East was selected by IDRC staff on the basis of their previous work on related issues. An effort was made to achieve the fairest possible representation from the various parts of the world, even though this criterion was secondary to that of relevant experience (Appendix 1 contains a list of the participants). Michel J. Menou, an international consultant in information management systems, was appointed by IDRC as the moderator of the conference. Participation in the conference was in a purely personal capacity, even though it did not preclude parallel contacts and discussions within the participants' communities or organizations.

To ensure the free expression of participants and to avoid possible delays and repetition as newcomers joined the proceedings, it was agreed the conference should be closed. Access to the full proceedings was restricted to the participants. Periodic summaries were prepared for use in personal communications with colleagues outside the conference.

On the basis of suggestions made by the participants, IDRC later identified a second group of 13 specialists with expertise and a keen interest in the theme of the conference to form a "consultative panel" (see Appendix 1). In many instances, they were specialists who might well have been included in the core group, but who either did not wish to or could not participate in the conference for various reasons, in particular through lack of adequate telecommunication facilities. Some members of this panel received a printed copy of the initial input and contributed comments to the conference as part of the personal contacts within the moderator's own network. Once the panel had been established by IDRC, toward the end of the conference, all members received, and were asked to comment on, printed copies of the summaries.

Participants were further encouraged to discuss freely the conference proceedings with colleagues and share their comments with other participants. To encourage this, the basic text of a press release was prepared at the beginning of the conference. At various times during the conference, it was sent by the moderator to 10 information science journals and newsletters and to a computer conference concentrating on information technology in developing countries (STIDEV on CoSy). In addition, announcements were published in the *Bulletin of the American Society for Information Science* (ASIS), the *ASIS Special Interest Group (SIG)/III Newsletter, Documentaliste-Sciences de l'Information,* and *La Lettre d'Inforcom* (Société Française des sciences de l'information et de la communication). Various professional meetings provided further opportunities for external contact. A number of information specialists expressed general interest in the conference theme and offered comments that were shared within the conference (see Appendix 1).

General comments about the project

The project was welcomed both within and outside the group of participants as an important, exciting, worthwhile, and timely endeavour. It was also expected to be a challenge because of the difficulty of devising criteria and a framework for assessing the impact of information on development. Discomfort was expressed because of the need to accommodate quite different and often incompatible concepts and perspectives, such as the "communication cycle" (King et al. 1976) versus "information economy"

(Machlup 1962). The lack of concrete data and the problem of gathering them were also perceived as major obstacles.

Reaching a better understanding of the role of information in development was nevertheless seen as a fundamental issue for the future of the information field. Although a focus on developing countries is legitimate in this respect, the same problems and questions hold for industrialized countries. A discussion of the effectiveness of current information systems and services and of the support granted to them could hardly be omitted from the project.

A number of external contributors, especially those from developing countries, criticized the relative underrepresentation of specialists from these countries in the core group of participants, although they acknowledged the practical obstacles to their involvement. They stressed that effective interaction at later stages of the project should be given the highest priority.

Similarly, the predominantly library and information science background of the core group of participants was questioned. Even at this early stage, some people thought that the inquiry would have benefited from participation by specialists in other fields, especially economics and development sociology, and by decision-makers in developing countries.

Despite the validity of these criticisms, the design options selected were deemed appropriate, especially in view of the exploratory nature of the project.

Structure and schedule of the conference

To facilitate interaction and the synthesis of the proceedings, the theme of the conference was broken down into 10 subthemes or topics: general, policies, benefits, indicators, calculation, field projects, research agenda, literature, others, and digests. A detailed description of their scope appears in Table 1.

On 6–8 April 1992, the conference began with a face-to-face meeting of the participants at IDRC headquarters in Ottawa,

Table 1. Subthemes in the computer conference.

Subtheme	Scope	Questions to be considered
General	Messages related to subjects bearing on the conference theme as a whole (theme, scope, objectives, overall approaches) or to several topics that could not be dealt with separately.	
Policies	Messages about the accountability of information policies vis-à-vis the identified benefits. Discussion in this area was not recommended until enough progress had been made on the subject of benefits.	How do the policy objectives of information programs and institutions, or other constituencies, and those mentioned in conjunction with activities related to the provision and use of information relate to identified overall benefits for society? How do the policy objectives of information programs and institutions, or other constituencies, and those mentioned in conjunction with activities related to the provision and use of information relate to identified overall benefits for society? Are the latter broad justifications of a rather theoretical nature or do they point to measurable results? What policy objectives would be geared to measurable benefits? Which conceptual framework (information infrastructure, information sector, information society) seems more favourable for the identification of appropriate policy objectives?
Benefits	Messages related to the discussion of benefits for whom. This topic was central to the conference and a priority for discussion.	What is the scope and nature of the benefits (economic, social, cultural, commercial, competitive, political, environmental) that can be expected to result from information activities? To what extent are the benefits associated with the evolution of the information infrastructure compatible with those resulting from the immediate provision of information services? Are some benefits more important than others? Do the negative side effects associated with the development of an information-intensive society offset the benefits?

(continued)

Table 1 continued.

Subtheme	Scope	Questions to be considered
Benefits (cont'd)		To what extent can the benefits resulting from information activities be compared to and assessed in the same way as those resulting from other kinds of nonmaterial production, such as education? Is it possible to identify benefits that are primarily a result of information activities independent of other conditions?
Indicators	Messages about the parameters or indicators by which the identified benefits can be assessed. Discussion in this area was not recommended until enough progress had been made on the topic of benefits.	Which facts could point to the achievement of the identified benefits? In what time frame can those facts be observed? What combination of facts is required to arrive at reliable assessments? Is it possible to assess short- and long-term benefits with the same set of parameters or indicators?
Calculation	Messages about suitable procedures for data gathering and calculation in relation ot the parameters or indicators selected. Discussion in this area was not recommended until enough progress had been made on the subjects of benefits and indicators.	What data are required to permit recognition of a particular benefit? How can these data be gathered? Can data gathering be incorporated into the routine operation of information services? How can indicators be calculated? To what extent should and could the proposed parameters or indicators allow for intercountry or international comparisons?
Field projects	Suggestions and discussion regarding future field testing or design of field projects that could incorporate the assessment of benefits. Discussion in the area was not recommended until enough progress had been made on the topics of benefits and indicators.	How could data gathering and monitoring of benefits be included among the components of the types of projects currently implemented in support of information activities? What other projects would need to be considered to facilitate such assessments? Are projects that are specifically geared toward the assessment of benefits required? If yes, what kinds of projects?

(continued)

Table 1 concluded.

Subtheme	Scope	Questions to be considered
Research agenda	Suggestions and discussion of future research that cannot be taken care of by field testing in conjunction with information projects. Such discussion was not recommended until enough progress had been made on the subjects of benefits and ndicators.	Which topics within the theme of the conference or in related areas would require a specific investigation? How could this investigation be carried out? Are there priorities among the proposed research topics? Can these activities be further specified at this stage?
Literature	Messages giving references and, if possible, short reviews especially for hard-to-access nonconventional material of relevant documents that all participants should be aware of.	
Others	This topic area was available for messages related to subjects such as ■ News from the participants (absence, travel, meetings); ■ Reporting on interactions within personal networks; ■ Comments on the proceedings and methods, suggestions for alteration of the conference structure and schedule; ■ CoSy and telecommunications procedures and problems; and ■ Other subjects that did not fit within the scope of the other conference topics.	
Digests	Periodic summaries of the proceedings and comments on them. The summaries themselves were "read only"; comments or requests for editing had to be presented in separate messages.	

Canada. The meeting was to allow members of the group to become acquainted and to establish the required group dynamics. It allowed participants to review the scope, objectives, agenda, and procedures for the conference. They also received basic training in the use of the CoSy computer conferencing system.

The computer conference was scheduled to take place over 5 months, from April through mid-September. IDRC provided the participants with technical support in relation to access to or use of the system as well as off-line communication channels in case of difficulties. Input received in printed form from external contributors was posted in the conference by the moderator.

Although all topics were open from the beginning, it was planned that the conference would proceed in steps. The structure, which had been approved in principle at the initial meeting, was tested during a trial period corresponding to the 1st month. The discussions were to concentrate on the various topics according to the following schedule:

- 1st and 2nd months: general, benefits, policy, and literature.
- 3rd month: benefits, policy, and indicators.
- 4th month: completing discussion of policy, benefits, and indicators; discussion of data gathering, field projects and research.
- 5th month: completing discussions on all topics.
- 6th month: preparation of the draft report.
- 7th month: discussion and revision of the draft report.

Participants were expected to contribute facts and ideas on each of the topics. This exercise was not meant as a formal international conference with balanced representation, diplomatic concerns, and corporate images to preserve. Except for the fact that each contribution had to be easily understood by all other participants, whose fluency in the conference language (English) might not match the sophistication of native speakers, there was no restraint upon free and thorough expression by all participants. "Crazy ideas" and iconoclastic contributions were indeed expected. To a large extent, the conference was seen an exercise in brainstorming. However, this did not exclude the eventual production of evidence, articulated justifications, or cases in point. In the meantime, because the conference was meant to achieve practical results (a conceptual framework, parameters or indicators, data-gathering procedures, project ideas, a research agenda), participants were urged to give due consideration to the applicability of their proposals under real-life conditions.

To facilitate interaction among the participants as well as with members of the consultative panel and external contributors, discussions on each topic would be synthesized by the moderator at regular intervals and as often as required.

Proceedings of the conference

The progress of the conference can be divided into four phases. Before the opening of the conference, 19 messages were posted under all the topics to provide a starting point for discussion. Because only six participants had an opportunity to interact through the conferencing system during the first month, the start-up phase was extended for one more month.

The second phase, covering the following 2 months, showed relatively slow progress with respect to both the number of active participants and the number of messages posted, which were mainly under General or Others. (This led to a decision to extend the conference for 2 months until mid-November.) Participants were then asked to avoid discussions under General, to focus on the subject of benefits for specific communities and problem areas, and to mention as far as possible the related indicators and data-gathering methods.

During the third phase (4th to 6th month), the conference reached what was considered its normal pace, with all participants establishing connections and using the system.

The last phase (7th and 8th months) was devoted to an overall review of the proceedings and last-minute input in the various topics.

From 20 November, messages in all topic areas were turned into "read only" files. Two new areas, one for substantive messages (report) and one for general announcements, were opened to allow for further interaction in the preparation of the final report and for submitting late input.

In all, 387 messages were posted: 96 under General, a number of them relating to alternative approaches to the assessment of benefits; 8 under Policies; 83 under Benefits; 26 under Indicators; 12 each under Calculation and Field Projects; 1 under Research Agenda; 17 under Literature; 98 under Others; and 34 under Digests. A substantial amount of unmonitored discussion also took place through person-to-person electronic mail. About 40% of the messages elicited at least one comment in the conference itself. Because of difficulties with telecommunications, the use of the system, and work pressure, seven participants contributed far fewer than the average number of messages.

A total of 24 messages were posted on behalf of 12 colleagues, who were either members of the consultative panel or external contributors. Half of these people provided messages under more than one topic. Two members of the consultative panel contributed five messages each.

Because the computer conference was conceived primarily as a brainstorming session among knowledgeable specialists, no systematic literature review was attempted. However, participants were invited to note and possibly comment on relevant documents. They are listed in the Bibliography, which covers documents noted as a result of this process, but is not a systematic bibliography on the subject. With the help of the IDRC Library, a number of online bibliographic searches were nevertheless attempted at the beginning of the conference. They did not provide significant results because of the peculiarity of the theme, for which consistent and specific indexing was difficult to identify, and because of the scatter of possibly relevant databases. The IDRC Library provided participants with copies of documents at their request. In addition, relevant material was circulated among the participants.

A summary of discussions at the initial meeting was not produced, because all but one participant was in attendance and most topics had been mentioned in a preliminary outline. A number of the messages posted during the 1st month did, in fact, offer some sort of summary on particular issues.

The production of summaries was based on the flow of messages and level of participation rather than following a predefined timetable. The first summary, covering 6 April to 6 July, was produced in mid-July along with some suggestions to the participants for achieving a better focus. Subsequent summaries covering 7 July to 9 September, 10 September to 6 October, and 7 October to 20 November were produced shortly after the covered period.

The moderator prepared a monthly review of the transactions, reporting the number of messages posted under each topic and the number of active participants. These reviews also included some guidance as to the focus of discussions for the forthcoming month.

After the close of the conference, between 21 November 1992 and the end of February 1993, 35 messages were exchanged among the participants, contributing to and commenting on the draft report. Most members of the consultative panel also offered comments. A number of electronic mail messages and letters were also exchanged and a few face-to-face discussions occurred. All comments were taken into account in revising the report.

Comments on the effectiveness of computer conferencing

In retrospect, different options for the design of the conference and its conduct, or additional features, might have led to greater and more effective participation. Although the design and implementation of this computer conference may have suffered from a number of deficiencies and inappropriate options, it nevertheless appears that the exercise was a valuable one and has brought about significant results that would not otherwise have been possible.

An independent evaluation of the computer conference as a

process for group investigation using this technology has suggested that it was a qualified success. The level of participation and interaction it achieved compares favourably with that encountered at face-to-face meetings. This is noteworthy in view of the lack of previous experience of most participants in the field of electronic communication. Although a comprehensive and accurate accounting for all aspects of the computer conference is not possible, the available data suggest that it was successful from a cost-effectiveness point of view as well.

Carefully designed computer conferences offer a unique opportunity for conducting investigations at an international level. Participants can, at their leisure, take as much time as they want to articulate their points and carry out any homework they deem appropriate. They can provide a comprehensive response to a series of contributions instead of replying spontaneously to one portion of a previous statement. They may submit material without interruption, delay, or distraction. The influence of individual roles, group reactions, and emotional perceptions are filtered. These advantages far outweigh the constraints, at least for people who are concerned with achieving a common goal rather than individual performance.

In addition to the technical, economic, and psychological limitations that were discussed at length in the literature on electronic communication, two obstacles to the full application of this technology must to be overcome. First, a minimum level of "computer literacy," especially the ability to handle electronic files and archives, is required. Second, ease of communication in an environment that is independent of distance and time cannot be regarded as a substitute for basic communication skills and a strong commitment to sharing ideas and participating in joint efforts. Overcoming these drawbacks requires appropriate training and the building of team spirit before embarking on a computer conference.

We hope that this technology will be increasingly available in all parts of the world. As it is more widely used and its application is monitored, we trust that it will produce the expertise that is needed to achieve its potential benefits fully.

Chapter 2

Background Considerations

———————■———————

Scope and focus
of the investigation

Initial discussions explored what is meant by "benefits" and their relation with the environment. We debated whether the project should first attempt to clarify basic concepts in this area or investigate a limited series of well-calibrated cases.

Several possible starting points were suggested:

- The impact of the various types of projects that support the development of information activities;

- The impact of roles and functions in the communication or information cycle on the achievement of development objectives;

- The impact of information on broad areas of information use (such as professional, educational, citizenship, social, domestic, cultural, and recreational);

- The impact of information in conjunction with specific activities related to the above areas of information use for specific constituencies characterized by location, group size, and level of education;

- The impact of information on specific sectors (such as legislature and overall political governance, public administration, research, education, social services, security, finance, trade, transport, communications, health services, other services, agriculture, forestry and fisheries, mining, manufacturing, energy, and environment); and

- The impact of information on major problem areas in development (such as satisfaction of basic needs, growth of GDP, improvement of trade balance, protection of the environment, debt control and reduction, industrialization, development of small enterprises, international competitiveness, modernization of the public sector, food security, human rights, people's participation, urban development, balanced demographic evolution, literacy, and women's status).

According to Vitro's (1990) "information sector hypothesis," development may be viewed as

> The ability of a society to add value to material and non material resources [which is] the key for generating local wealth and an important factor in contributing to a more equitable distribution of new wealth. To add value is to add to the information content of resources.

Production factors and the main areas of benefit could form the rows and columns of a basic matrix; at the intersections, one could try to identify specific benefits, expressed in terms of value added or otherwise, that could be considered as primarily resulting from the provision and use of information. The matrix itself could be considered successively in conjunction with each of the facets of information use, possibly combined with relevant types of information activities or roles and functions on different scales from individual to large groups.

The factors of production to be considered are human resources, materials, technology (machines and processes), and money. Other important parameters, like markets, time, environment, organizations, and social structures, should also be examined. The following areas of potential benefit, and possibly others, could be considered:

- Quantitative increase in production;
- Qualitative increase in production;

- Level of sophistication or innovation (this refers to new or enhanced products or processes, whereas the two previous areas refer to existing ones);

- Appropriateness (better response to needs);

- Reduction in adverse side effects;

- Greater viability (minimization of failures);

- Completeness (ability to cope with complexity);

- Autonomy (ability to operate with minimal external support and guidance, ability to resist undue pressures);

- Self-reliance (especially in an international context); and

- Competitiveness (alignment on national and international standards of cost-effectiveness).

Special attention must be paid to the possible effect of the use of information on the limitations inherent in conditions in developing countries. Examples of such limitations include relative remoteness from major markets and decision centres, social and cultural heterogeneity, institutional instability, and insecurity of financial resources.

Although it may be necessary for practical purposes, it is questionable whether specific uses of information (professional, recreational, educational) should be dealt with separately or considered in combination for particular constituencies and problems, such as the use of popular drama for disseminating social, economic, or technical information. The contribution of information to development at a global, national, or regional level is often referred to and must be elucidated. However, it seems that reliable assessments at this level are almost beyond reach.

Some participants believed that the starting point should be the users, more specifically the end users of information. A distinction could be made between those who actually use information or are likely to do so and potential users who are not likely, for a number of reasons, to turn themselves into actual users during the period of the investigation. Some participants believe that the latter may be disregarded in assessing the impact of information. One may then focus on those for whom the availability of information is likely to induce a behavioural change and result in actions that will have a significant impact on their well being and, thus, possibly on development. In this respect, both formal and semi-structured groups and small enterprises play a fundamental role (Salmona 1981). Assessing the function of information in the actions of these development actors is possible; it might be much harder to find out if, and to what extent, their actions have an impact on development.

A reasonable consensus was reached in discussions to remain with micro-scale projects, clusters of projects, or sectors leaving the macro level to "theologians." However a certain level of aggregation is required to take into account a number of external factors. To achieve this, it may be appropriate to concentrate on a few critical situations or "information use environments" (see Chapter 4 for a description of this notion).

A series of models embedding well-delineated types of information, socioeconomic goals, and specific environments and information-use parameters may facilitate analysis. A major emphasis in these models could be an attempt to trace how information contributes to the enhancement of the activities of the various categories of development actors in relation to the critical aspects of development or major problem areas, such as those depicted by development indicators.

A further approach may be to select two countries known for their relatively "good" and "bad" performance in a given area, such as health, and study the use and impact of information provision in the concerned constituencies. Such comparisons would need to be based upon averaged measures of factors directly related to the target activities.

Other key parameters involve the time span for any investigation and the scale of benefits. Is the accumulation of short-term or individual benefits likely to result in long-term or global benefits? It is also unclear whether benefits are likely to be the same in the short, medium, and long term or whether benefits derived from the support of infrastructure are similar to and compatible with benefits derived from the more immediate provision of information services.

There are objections in principle to the various ways of grouping and differentiation among countries on the basis of their economic development level, assumed information development level, size, or other categorization. However, developing countries differ widely. Economic development level may be used as one parameter. At least, once potential benefits have been identified, one should specify for which types of countries they are deemed valid and whether they can apply to other types of countries or to all.

Indicators: for whom and for what purpose?

Indicators shall be used to provide justification for information activities, especially to policymakers. It may be appropriate to specify who will use the proposed indicators as a basis for selecting the cases to be investigated. It may be important to determine how to attract the attention of these users, which argument they are sensitive to, what level of detail they are likely to expect in the indicators, what factual evidence of the returns or impact they expect, what decisions are expected from them, and what arguments will convince them.

To the extent that donor agencies have played a major role in information development, it could be helpful to know whether they have identified constituencies that are more aware of the benefits of information and more willing to take action accordingly, and whether they pay more attention to certain types of information activities or particular benefits. Because, at least in the formal information sector, the achievement of benefits depends on the activities of the information specialists who will participate in their assessment, the indicators should also be meaningful and acceptable to them.

Causality

To some extent, indicators are expected to demonstrate a causal relation between information and development and quantify the related phenomena. It is premature to ask whether information "causes" development or, conversely, development "causes" information. This might even be a false problem. Earlier studies (such as Lau 1988) seem to indicate that once a minimal degree of satisfaction of basic needs has been achieved, the growth of information resources and their use does not occur solely in conjunction with further accumulation of wealth, but may be comparatively faster in communities or nations that place a higher emphasis on this resource, both in cultural and policy terms.

Causal links are difficult to establish because of the complexity of real-life situations in contemporary societies and of the number of noninformation-related internal and external factors associated with any endeavour. Furthermore, short-term benefits are more information intensive. In assessing long-term benefits, information use is combined with so many external factors that its relative impact is difficult to identify.

Thus, one may find evidence that better performance occurs when information is effectively used and, conversely, performance is poorer when it is not. This relation may be enough to support the idea that information is a necessary condition for, or ingredient of, development and causal links may not be required at this stage. A number of studies (Strassmann 1985, 1990; Koenig 1990) suggest that such a relation exists. Determining the impact of information is no less complex an endeavour. Good information projects or processes may have no impact, or even a negative one, because other required inputs are absent; bad projects or processes may have a positive impact because of favourable external factors.

No specific factor, much less information, can be singled out as a main cause of development. A wide range of external influences are involved at each level in the assessment of the impact of information. It may thus be more important to find out which benefits are primarily associated with information if, indeed, "primarily" can be defined.

The quest for a causal relation between information and development implies, to some extent, that decision-making is rational and based upon some sort of cost–benefit analysis. However, decisions may be based on a rationale that differs from this and other theories of decision-making. They may even result from a combination of rationales or of drives that would be perceived as "irrational" by external observers.

The need to link benefits with costs

Benefits cannot be assessed without considering the cost of providing the services that may generate them. Benefits must also be weighed against costs in justifying the continuation of information provision. However, some benefits, such as increased autonomy or rationality, can hardly be related to any particular information resource and, thus, cost.

To the extent that the supply side and its costs are relatively better known, a possible approach might be to begin by identifying potential benefits, assuming cost-effective provision and use of information services. Once potential benefits have been identified, we can specify the infrastructure and services necessary for them to materialize, then calculate their cost. Finally, we can estimate the value of the benefits and compare it with the cost of providing the information.

The cost of providing and using information is difficult to compute, especially in nonformal systems or formal ones that are not thoroughly structured. This situation limits the extent to which cost–benefit analysis can be applied in this field. However, properly designed and conducted cost–benefit analyses have proved to be both feasible and promising.

Development

There is a lack of consensus regarding the concept of "development" (for example, growth of gross national product (GNP) versus distribution of wealth). "Development" and "information" must be defined from the viewpoint of developing countries. Participants in the computer conference acknowledged the problem. They felt that it would be unrealistic to expect any authoritative definition. They stressed, however, that any impact assessment should state explicitly the particular point of view on which it is based. "Economic development" may be less difficult to pin down than "development." For a country with a high GNP per capita, development may relate to quantitative and possibly qualitative growth, but does not imply much structural change; in a country with a low GNP per capita, structural changes are almost inevitably a requisite.

A capacity for development is enhanced through the simultaneous cultivation of material and nonmaterial resources. Development requires strengthening the infrastructure for cultivating physical resources (land, material, plants, and energy) and intellectual or creative resources (those that build human capital). By raising the value of human capital, a dynamic society is capable of sustainable economic development. "Development, even economic development, is a knowledge based process" (Boulding 1966).

A number of "development indicators" are currently used to trace significant changes in the evolution of modern societies: urbanization, literacy, vocational training, newspaper circulation, political democracy, independent judiciary, free enterprise, rational behaviour, social mobility, occupational diversity, associations, fewer factions (ethnic or other), and nuclear families. Clusters of indicators, such as the "human development indicators" or "quality of life indicators," have also been used. They may indicate areas in which a search for a particular impact of information may be worthwhile.

Many so-called development indicators and the value judgements based upon them seem to equate development with the replication of socioeconomic structures found in the Northern Hemisphere. Efforts to devise more appropriate indicators, such as the quality of life indicator developed by Morris (1979), the socioeconomic indicators compiled by the United Nations Research Institute for Social Development, or, more recently, the human development indicators produced by the United Nations Development Programme (UNDP 1992), have aimed at providing a more accurate picture. Beyond data availability and calculation methods, the conceptual framework that underlies such assessments remains a critical issue. Gross national happiness may be opposed to gross national product.

Is there a significant difference between "knowledge" and "information" in the development process, referring, for instance, to IDRC's concept of "empowerment through knowledge" (IDRC 1991) and considering the classical distinctions between data, information, and knowledge? One may contend that there definitely is a difference and even that true development can only be manifested by wisdom, the final stage in data transformation. A community that is highly advanced, with regard to its material wealth and technological capacity, and information rich can be predatory and ultimately self-destructive, as evidenced by many examples in history.

Criteria for wisdom are not necessarily universal and may not apply beyond the individual; but, by any yardstick, most contemporary societies have a long way to go before they achieve it. Nevertheless, the issue of a "knowledge society" versus an "information society" has recently emerged and is getting increased attention; it may be of particular relevance to the theme of the conference. If information is "organized data which are (or rather can be) communicated" (Porat and Rubin 1977), knowledge is information that has been meaningfully aggregated into a reservoir of facts and concepts that can be applied — that is, information that has been absorbed or "appropriated." As a result, the endogenous information and knowledge, rather than the "world's store of information" and access to it, should be regarded as the main source of potential benefits.

To some extent, the notion of wisdom, when applied to large communities, like nations, is quite close to the one of "social intelligence" (Dedijer and Jequier 1988). In this approach, however, the effectiveness of the behaviour of the considered communities tends to be assessed within the existing socioeconomic and ideological structures that now dominate the world. One wonders whether wisdom would not also include the ability to reconsider those fundamental structures themselves when they do not meet the expectations of humankind or prove unable to overcome intrinsic contradictions.

Information

Contrary to the hopes expressed in the literature of the 1950s and 1960s, information is no magic recipe for development. The alleged key role of information in development is based upon three assumptions that are not fully, if at all, verified:

- Potential information users are capable of rational choices based upon cost–benefit analysis or similar logical processes;

- There is perfect information; and

- Access to information has no cost.

Information has indeed a direct cost for all users, even if it is not apparent. More importantly, incentives to adopt new techniques or behaviour matter more than the dissemination of information about them. Information can have a negative impact on development if it is not associated with structural changes (Samarajiva 1989).

According to Mackenzie-Owen (1992), "information has a value-in-use, or potential value," that can be assessed only "after it has been used and its results have become viable." Information systems and infrastructures have a value added that is expressed by the efficiency and effectiveness of their delivery of information (availability and usability) and the improvements in the attributes of information-as-contents, as well as in their delivery mechanisms. Many information producers and providers have little idea about the value-in-use of information for their clients and not much more about the value added of their services. The value of information may lie more in its versatility (its applicability to a variety of problems, even unanticipated ones) than in its straight application to the activities for which it was originally meant.

Because of its characteristics, information may not be managed like other production factors. This may partly explain why the focus is currently on information technology rather than on information itself. Are there basic (consumption) needs for information as there are for food, shelter, and health?

Attention tends to be focused on the positive role of information and its contribution to enlightenment. However, it might also contribute to conservatism if it transfers "what has existed in the past" through traditional channels. This effect may result from the lack of a problem-solving attitude in information use (for example, see Slamecka 1982). Information may be sought to justify decisions that have already been made, rather than to provide input for innovative solutions, or to reinforce "irrational" decisions in some instances.

Regarding the situation in developing countries, two categories of information should be considered:

- Endogenous information (produced or elaborated within the country) and

- Exogenous information (produced in and retrieved from other countries).

Respect for and expansion of the local knowledge base are essential in promoting science, technology, and their applications by a society in ways that are consistent with its needs, conditions, resources, and aspirations. Traditional wisdom must be blended with external information and expertise. Because of the monopoly of technostructure in the communication cycle and the manipulation of endogenous information by governments, preference is often given to exogenous information by users outside and even inside the technostructure.

Content, activity, and commodity are three sets of aspects to be distinguished when considering the impact of information. The information itself, considered for its content, is a resource; the processes and channels through which it is exchanged are activity; and its packaging is a commodity. Developing countries should also consider information as a commodity, especially with respect to the international market; they should find ways to package information into an exportable commodity.

"Raw" or unprocessed information (like biological information, such as the properties of plants) represents a potential wealth for developing countries. About 25% of medicines currently in use originated from plants. If the revenue derived from the patented processes used in the extraction of their active components is not shared with the communities that are responsible for preserving their habitat, these communities will have no incentive and are often not in a position to continue this preservation (Vogel 1991). Raw materials are obtained for a minimal price, often taking further advantage of cheap labour; the end products are sold for considerable profit, thus aggravating economic imbalances and the risk of exhausting the resource. To some extent, raw information is "latent." It is loosely organized and not ready to be communicated, but its potential value may be high. The recent debates on biodiversity, leading up to the Convention on Biological Diversity of the Rio Earth Summit, or patentability of the biological properties of endogenous species show that this resource is real.

Information in all its forms can be found in both formal and informal structures. The informal information sector is likely to play a far more important role in developing countries. Great caution should be taken to avoid equating, consciously or not, information to what is available in the formal sector. Unstructured, informal, spontaneous, and personal information is so deeply rooted in the cultural context of developing countries that none of the assessment models created for formal or technical information applies. Excluding culturally determined information processes and products from a conceptualization of the "information society" to be analyzed in a search for indicators would produce a defective picture. In countries where rural development and the strengthening of local enterprises, small organizations, farms, cooperatives, and local government are national goals, the impact of information dissemination cannot be assessed without accepting the influence of local cultures.

Sociocultural influences

The value of information depends on users' attitudes and behaviour vis-à-vis the information. Its availability alone does not change behaviour. The willingness of users to change, their ability to interpret information, and the credibility of the information are key factors in this respect. The sociocultural context in which many decision-makers currently operate may not be conducive to information use, for example, when any increase in production by farmers is likely to be outweighed by additional taxes. Conversely, the intensive use of parallel, nonformal, information sources in crisis situations, even at risk of life, shows that information is indeed regarded as a critical resource.

The term "decision-maker" is used here in a broad sense and does not refer exclusively to those in charge of organizations, but to any person or group having to make a decision to solve a particular problem. Being informed without being in a position to take corrective action is useless. Thus, some decision-makers may prefer to use lack of information as a ready excuse. Moreover, the elite may have access to the other factors needed to make effective use of information, while the poor do not. It would be interesting to find out whether the "informal sector" is more information rich than the formal sector, for example.

Decision-making and problem-solving, especially with respect to broad issues, are not only logical, but also emotional, irrational, or simply inspired. Nonformal and nonconscious information influences the interpretation and application of formal information. In addition, information fulfills irrational and symbolic functions whose value or contribution to the performance of organizations and people requires research. The interference from emotions seems to keep pace with the availability of information. As more and more information is produced, many people have less and less of the information they need when they need it or are in a position to harness it.

For information to be used effectively, it may need to be attuned to the traditional communication patterns. But tradition may also be a strong factor in resistance to any form of progress; for example, access to knowledge may be considered a sin. For some people, the only solution to this dilemma is to break with tradition completely. Others believe that a synthesis between tradition and modern practices, to occur in the medium term, may provide the solution to this contradiction (Logelin 1992).

In addition to the values of users, the perceptions of information specialists, or intermediaries, of benefits and their own value systems are factors that affect the provision and use of information. In cultures where information is highly controlled (usually creating an underground information market), information professionals often act, or are perceived as acting, as barriers to information use. For example, they may restrict access or be considered the custodians of "official," biased information. They have no incentive to reach potential users beyond the narrow circle of predetermined authorized users.

An interesting issue is the importance placed on internally generated information. In many countries, irrespective of their level of development, such information often has to fit within traditionally accepted or "official" formats and preconceptions. The accuracy of the endogenous information may thus be questioned by many. In some instances, it may even be forced into a system of thought or representation that relies more upon magic than logic (for example, the one-time quest for "authenticity" or the claim that a problem is "an invention of imperialism"). It may lack the structured ideology and systematism that made official discourse in socialist countries, for instance, more usable or dependable, at least in its own sphere of validity. In such situations, real information is sought, even by high-ranking officials, from informal channels or rumours and external sources that may be no less biased; this situation is reflected, for instance, in the general reverence for reports from international organizations.

All information, even scientific data, may be culturally biased. "There is not one logic but many logics. Aristotelian logic is not *the* scientific logic" (Maruyama 1974).

"Power games" exert a significant influence in both the national and international arenas. At both levels, self-determination and fair access to information should certainly be regarded as critical benefits.

In the rational arena, more educated and informed people are likely to be more effective; they are also likely to be less obedient. The desire for betterment as a result of information is balanced by fear of loss of the easy control that an information-poor environment allows. When information reaches the masses, it may put the established authorities at risk in many developing countries and others as well. Information is under the control of governments that use it as a tool to maintain power, resulting in distrust of public information by the masses and lack of faith in the specialists who are responsible for its delivery.

In the international arena, there is a widespread feeling in the South that the North wishes to preserve its control of "the tree of knowledge" and maintain the South as an exporter of raw information. There is alleged pressure from the North to force its information technology and products on the South regardless of their appropriateness. The North also resists recognizing the rights of the South over the raw information contained in its natural resources and sharing the technology required to turn it into formal information, as evidenced during the 1992 Earth Summit in Rio de Janeiro. The South is faced with a dilemma: whether to cut itself off from the North and develop endogenous information or to establish, as quickly as possible, modern information facilities closely connected with those in the North.

Information policies

For most constituencies, whether formal or not, information is not yet perceived as a factor distinguishable from the activities in which it is involved. When it is a recognized issue, the perception of information and appropriate policies that apply to it vary between two extremes. At one end, the concept of information sector is seen as too broad and vague; rather, its specific components should be considered when attempting to define objectives. At the other extreme, it is thought that no single segment of the information sector can compete with the other, better established sectors for scarce resources.

Many specialists believe that modern information infrastructure requires inputs and maintenance that are too costly for developing countries. This kind of information is probably not what they require most. Its role in development is overemphasized by the North, which seeks to open markets for its products.

No positive, explicit mention of a possible contribution of information to development, beyond the established cliché, could be traced in the statements justifying most information-related programs and policies in developing countries. The expected benefits are expressed in such broad and general terms that it is difficult to translate them into potential, observable results. They are eventually referred to as a "basic human right," thus implicitly being beyond any objective assessment.

In some cases, information projects indicate potential benefits, such as saved time, more timely decisions, and avoidance of unnecessary duplication of activities, but they seldom offer relevant data about the initial situation or provide for monitoring the achievement of such benefits.

Information systems, services, and infrastructure

Given the current inadequacy of formal information infrastructure, systems, and services, can benefits be identified? Examining benefits implies concomitant consideration of the changes necessary on the supply side. Information encompasses both content and the process by which it is transmitted; the two aspects must be distinguished. For the various categories of users, it might be appropriate to ask what information (content) is likely to contribute to development and how its delivery can be organized or improved.

Information infrastructure, especially in developing countries, is often considered to restrict rather than enable the flow of information. Investment is concentrated in the central part of organizations or in major cities. The system primarily serves narrow groups or privileged people. Access to information is selective and often subject to various forms of "censorship." (It is appropriate to reflect upon the wealth of formal information being accumulated in the industrialized countries that is underused, despite significant investment and promotion.)

Should information infrastructure serve the poor or the elite? Access to all information resources by everyone might be regarded as a basic principle or long-term objective, but cost-effective ways to implement this principle are much less evident, particularly in an information-poor environment. The reality and extent of the alleged multiplier effect attached to providing information to the elite needs to be investigated, especially when no significant change in the established power structure or the functional arrangement of organizations is associated with it. A balance must be achieved between the application of modern information technology, on the one hand, and local conditions for its proper operation, traditional communication patterns, and the information needs of the masses, on the other. The lack of true national languages, multiplicity of local languages, and illiteracy are grossly overlooked in the design of information and communication systems and more so in national planning of information and communication.

The personnel involved in providing information services seem to be convinced that information is essential and pay little attention to short-term returns. They blame lack of support and the ignorance of users for the limited effectiveness of their services. Their low status and poor career prospects result in a high turnover, lack of motivation, and poor quality of service. To maximize value, it seems more appropriate to create an information-rich environment than to try to provide information on demand. Information needs are difficult to identify in advance and the cost, in terms of money and time, of generating and packaging information in response to ad hoc requests is high.

Information development support

Support for information development is relatively scarce and sparse compared with support for other development activities. These limitations add to the difficulty of assessing the impact of information on development, especially at the national level. In addition, there is much duplication among donors, communication in this area is poor, and there is not enough cross-fertilization with regard to information, ideas, and experiences.

Donors seem to rely on rules of thumb in choosing objectives and priorities for information projects. Information development support seeks a balance between the development of infrastructure and the satisfaction of the information needs of the poorest segments of the population (Samarajiva and Shields 1990). The latter, like rural populations, are mainly reached by indirect methods, usually through extension services. When resources are scarce, choices between infrastructure and serving the poor are often in favour of the former.

The information professions may also be blamed for being unable to offer a rationale for the cost–benefit of information provision and use compared with other forms of development support. Studying the advantages of providing information versus health inspections or vaccination campaigns, for example, may reveal useful insights.

Assessments in other fields and their application

Participants agreed that the project could benefit from an examination of the methods and findings of similar impact assessments in other fields, whether material, such as transport or telecommunications, mixed, such as tourism, or immaterial, such as science and technology or education. The criteria and ratios used by large corporations in deciding to invest in continuing education and information support could also provide a useful example. General development indicators and the actual measures used might be a source of inspiration, at least with regard to calculation methods.

Studies have been made of the correlation between the level of socioeconomic development and information use, size of the information sector, or incidence of information activities (see Menou 1985). However, the researchers relied upon indicators that are tied to material goods, they were not able to reach clear conclusions, and they concentrated more on the availability of information than on its specific role and impact.

Investigations that sought to establish irrefutable relations between investment in information technology or information and the effects of its use, especially on productivity, have generally failed to do so. Their failure has not necessarily been due to the quality of research or the rigour of the models; it has resulted from the very nature of the socioeconomic and cultural environment in which information is produced, distributed, and used. Some argue that measuring tools are to blame, others that investment strategies have aggravated organizational, economic, and other problems. As a result, policymakers remain unpersuaded, although selected indicators and models have had an incremental effect on the views of people in government and industry.

It was suggested that some of the findings of the Trilateral Group (Canada, United Kingdom, and USA), which is studying the role of information in the economy might be useful (Trilateral Group 1988). However, its discussions concentrated on basic issues without specifically considering assessments or indicators. At its June 1992 meeting, the Trilateral Group commissioned a review of the major systems of definition, measurement, and classification that might inhibit the understanding and exploitation of the role of information in the economy. The timing for this exercise did not allow our conference to benefit from its possible input.

Economics and information sciences have been struggling for decades to identify criteria for the assessment and measurement of the impact of information. Several promising models for decision-making have been created and cast aside. Each offered a useful approach for considering certain types of information, but each was limited. The exclusive attention of decision-makers to return on investment may be a major constraint in considering the benefits resulting from information. For example, the model of decision-making in the firm has cast a long shadow on the conceptualization of information by focusing on structured, formal, and technical information; it ignored unstructured, informal, spontaneous, and personal information.

Qualitative evaluation models may be identified in development science, rural sociology, communication science, and education rather than in economics. The trend toward creating and evaluating models of the local impact and sustainability of development that began in the late 1960s has produced numerous interesting paradigms that might be worth examining.

Research on information theory may also be of use. The measures of impact already developed to a considerable extent in bibliometrics, scientometrics, and informetrics might have some relevance here, although it is questionable whether citation implies usage and usage means impact on development. Some aspects of the management sciences (decision support systems, management information systems, and executive information systems) could be relevant. Lessons might also be found in the judiciary and the legal process, which depend heavily on the use of information.

Indicators to measure the impact of education have been developed over more than 20 years, especially in Latin America, where four or five countries are now proficient in this field. In one report, the indicators were based upon a cost–benefit analysis of human capital building. They appeared to be convincing enough to justify investments in education and, therefore, to have a visible effect. However, apparently, there is a lack of skilled strategic analysts who can make proper use of such indicators. What has been learned from efforts to devise indicators in research and planning has not been absorbed by administrators. Assimilation has been gradual and resistance to change has been strong. Doubts about the evidence provided by the indicators still prevail in many areas.

The Society of Competitive Intelligence Professionals (SCIP) is also addressing the question of return on investment and grappling with similar problems in convincing management of the benefits of corporate intelligence departments by demonstrating and measuring returns. To this end, it has established an ideas clearinghouse.

Chapter 3

BENEFITS

———————•———————

Benefits for whom?

Although the problem of how to prove that information is an essential resource has existed for a long time, no one has been able to solve it, at least in general terms. This may be because it cannot be solved in general terms. It seems almost impossible to identify general benefits and their related indicators, as the concept, nature, and goals of development may differ from one person to another, from one time to another, and from one situation to another.

Concentrating on the global level or using it as a starting point to work down to lower levels is a practice fraught with problems. A common mistake made in evaluating projects is collecting data at a level that is too general. Lower level data are needed to interpret higher level trends. Another problem that arises at the global or national level is that information varies enormously in its value among different sectors — not having the right information at the right time can have much more serious consequences in some fields (an emergency in a nuclear reactor) than in others (the choice of a handpump for a water supply and sanitation scheme). In addition, local goals and objectives may not be the same as more general ones, because of the need to address immediate concerns.

However, local (or immediate) problem-solving or decision-making might improve if considered in a broader context and with regard to effects on large-scale, long-term objectives and goals. Also, although local needs may not seem the same as global ones, decisions or actions at this level may have consequences that affect national benefits, either positively or negatively. Because what is good for one community may be bad for another, national benefits are not necessarily the sum of local ones. A clear picture at the micro level is a prerequisite, but an unconstrained validation at the macro level may prove more than useful. For particular areas, outlining national benefits before attempting to identify local benefits may be appropriate.

Producing a comprehensive, authoritative encyclopedia of benefits and related indicators for information activities and projects in developing countries was thought to be, if not impossible, then of limited value, because indicators depend on context and, thus, their number is infinite. However, identifying as many potential benefits as possible and producing a systematic, open-ended list might be a desirable long-term goal, particularly if it would guide local specialists to develop indicators for specific purposes.

Rather than considering the impact of information on development, one should look at its impact on the goals and objectives, decisions and actions, intellectual equipment, and overall skills of precisely identified categories of the population in relation to their most critical problems. For example, one might select a set of development goals, such as improving health care and raising the level of employment and average income, then try to link them with the intermediate objectives necessary to achieve these goals (such as adequate health care personnel, facilities, and investment in primary health care infrastructure).

Because the many issues cannot be covered comprehensively, priorities should be set in terms of constituencies, environments, and problems. Those that seem most promising for demonstrating an effect or most challenging for understanding the relationship between information and development can be chosen, so that even preliminary responses to these problems might be proposed. For a specific development goal, like improved health care or food production, hundreds, or even thousands, of intermediate objectives can be identified. One can then determine who contributes to these objectives and how, and then find out how information contributes to the activities of the identified groups.

Benefits and value are now believed to be determined by users and use, rather than by processing "raw materials." Quality is thus being defined in terms of the user's net comparative value of the good or service.

Benefits may be bound to the expansion of the endogenous knowledge base, including integration of exogenous information. This benefit depends on the capacity of the system, mainly the human portion, to absorb information. Case studies of problem-solving related to critical development issues may both illustrate the realization of benefits and provide a basis for developing learning material that would enhance the capacity to absorb.

Should personal benefits, especially for the people associated with the governance of institutions or management of organizations, be taken into account even though they may be contrary to benefits for the community and thus unethical? This issue may be even broader. Should one consider any benefit, even if it may seem unethical on whatever ground?

Benefits from what?

In our information-intensive society, the most important assistance that information specialists can provide is information itself and the skills to use information more effectively to work more intelligently. Measuring the effect of these functions is part of our challenge.

The oral tradition, which has been overlooked by information scientists, continues to be a vital component of many cultures. Definitions of communication must accommodate the importance of nonwritten traditions and the transfer of informal information in addition to structured technical information. The best formal information systems can easily be bypassed by an effective, informal network. Measures and policies should recognize and reflect this.

A "visual tradition" is replacing the oral or written ones in many cultures, or at least heavily supplementing it. In industrialized countries, an entire generation (now moving into a second one) was raised with television, videos, and computer games. These people get their information and entertainment from still and moving images more often than the printed word. The new media and information technologies, combined with urbanization, or rather "megapolization," and other social changes propel us toward a "brave new world" rather than to a new form of oral tradition, because they lack the interpersonal trust on which traditional exchange is based. A "global virtual reality" is being created in which manipulation of all types becomes possible. Carbo Bearman (1992) describes the need for a new kind of literacy that she calls "mediacy" to denote the need for skill in using multimedia information sources effectively and to connote the immediacy of information delivery (such as via satellite). New concepts and designs are also needed for information systems that fully incorporate and adjust to these dimensions.

The following aspects of the provision of information were noted as being worth special consideration with regard to their effect on value and benefits:

- Trade-offs between timeliness and accuracy of information;

- Changing information strategies within private and public organizations with new "enterprise" orientations;

- "Commoditization" of information;

- Information rich versus information poor;

- Human, organizational, and technological capability of using information; and

- Demands for information from intergovernmental organizations and aid donors.

The concept of information resources management (IRM) may prove particularly attractive for developing countries. Interest has already been noted, but no authoritative research has been done that would help them understand and apply the concept to their special and unique circumstances. IRM seems to be confined to only scattered enclaves outside of the Western world.

Further to the IRM concept, information can and should be regarded in organizational contexts (especially large and complex organizations) as a resource. They should be planned for, managed, and controlled like any other resource. However, resources differ and, therefore, the techniques and tools used to manage one resource may not be directly applicable to another. The specific policies and principles used to manage information resources must take into account the similarities and differences between information resources and the other resources. Information resources include sources, systems, services, and networks, and may be manual or automated or a mixture of the two.

Functionally, an IRM program must address such issues as organizational structure, leadership, tools, information audits, and information "bench-marking." More specifically, the process must manage the knowledge workers, the information infrastructure, the information delivery system, and the ultimate users to ensure that they are sufficiently skilled to apply the information effectively and efficiently to achieve results. The information management process must answer five questions:

- What knowledge is worthwhile?

- Who in the organization has or should have it?

- Who should receive this knowledge? Why? What are they expected to do with it?

- How can we improve the way we collect and disseminate existing knowledge?

- How can we improve the way in which we create new knowledge that is needed by using more creative techniques?

An organization that does not practice IRM does not address these challenges in a comprehensive and systematic manner. Rather, it operates implicitly believing that people should be their own "information experts" and need no outside help. It also believes that information is a vague, amorphous abstraction that cannot be addressed in any scientific way. It believes that serendipity is the only way new knowledge is discovered. If this view were extrapolated, then everyone should be their own doctor, lawyer, and accountant. Some may cope with these functions, at least in part; but most people need professional help. In contrast, IRM proponents believe that the information professional is an emerging, bona fide professional that all organizations need — especially large and complex ones.

Any evidence of substantial information brokerage in developing countries should alert us to the value placed on information by the communities served by these activities. The development of information companies may result in employment opportunities. Their services also provide direct benefits to their customers and possible indirect and long-term ones if they contribute to a better understanding by the users of the value of information. Demand and sales may be used as surrogates for broader and more difficult to discern benefits.

Fee-based services and progress toward self-supporting information services in the government sector, or privatization, may have the same effect. There is an urgent need to explore this avenue. However, for now, information services in developing countries are mostly in the public sector and are available without charge. Users have no funds earmarked for the purchase of information and may not have the required resources. Alternative strategies and a shift in subsidies between supply and demand may need to be considered. Current conditions may restrict enquiry to the modern sector and to formal information services.

A comparative analysis of investments in information transfer and technology transfer in selected developing countries might also be considered. Focusing on information as an integrative tool for development should prove particularly valuable in Africa and the Caribbean where small countries must "team up" to initiate and sustain meaningful development. In this respect, one should examine the cost of transborder flow of data and information compared with such flow between each country and its former colonial masters and the value-added properties of information in time and space.

Creating an information-rich environment is a critical, long-term benefit. It would result in more diversity, flexibility, and versatility in the information resources, more reliable information, wider use by more categories of users, and more integrated and more standardized services. These types of benefits cannot be assessed in terms of cost per library visit, information search, or any user transaction.

Benefits resulting from the creation of an information-rich environment may be observed, as far as the formal information sector is concerned, in enhancements to the infrastructure, such as increased capabilities, better products and services, better data integrity and reliability, wider and more intensive use, better application of information in decision-making, more intensive exchanges, more cooperation among the units involved in all steps of the communication cycle, and development of labour.

Benefits derived from cultural or recreational use of information should not be neglected. They are expected by people. They relate to a number of actual information projects. The particular roles or needs of the individual — as producer, consumer, or citizen — cannot be separated from the others. The patterns of cross-fertilization among the various uses of information are not known.

To the extent that government-sponsored development studies, and others, are primarily investments in the generation of knowledge and information, one might consider the circumstances in which their outcomes are used. Similarly, the development plans of various developing countries could be used to learn how information is used at the various stages: formation and rejection of ideas, planning, implementation, and evaluation. As mentioned in the previous chapter, raw information contained in natural resources and latent information not yet properly organized for communication may be important sources of potential benefits for developing countries.

There may be "normal" and "abnormal" scenarios for development. A normal development scenario may be one in which the legislative, executive, and judicial branches of the government each play their respective role. One might determine the use of information in each branch and examine if a "normal scenario" can occur when one of the three branches functions suboptimally or is subsumed under one of the other two, as in a military dictatorship, thus leading to an "abnormal scenario."

Types of benefits

Saracevic (1980) may have been wrong in claiming that there is no empirical evidence that information plays a fundamental role in development. Consider what happens when one takes away information, or when one provides no training or poor training of personnel. Saracevic probably meant that there is no *quantitative* evidence, or that it is not systematically consolidated.

Three broad classes of impact can be distinguished: those that are both measurable and quantifiable, such as cost and time savings; those that are measurable but not quantifiable, such as increased quality; and those that are neither measurable nor quantifiable, such as new insights, learning, and performance of higher-order tasks (up-scaling).

Two main categories of benefits relate to the nature or area of application of the changes resulting from the use of information:

- Direct benefits, which are an immediate consequence of using information for the purpose for which it was sought, to solve the particular problem for which it was sought; and

- Indirect benefits, which may only occur in the medium or long term and are not specifically related to the problem at hand when the information was used (for example, structuring the knowledge base, enlightenment, and attitudinal changes).

In each of these categories, two subcategories can be further distinguished based on the conditions of occurrence of the benefits:

- Immediate benefits, which can occur in the short term and as a direct effect of the availability of information. They can be observed and they express the most evident impact or effect of information products and services (costs and benefits or counter-benefits) and of the use of resources required to generate the information products and services (costs and benefits of information provision).

■ Potential benefits, which require other conditions to be fulfilled. They may arise if certain conditions are met to allow successful use of the information in a given context. These benefits are likely to be more remote and realized in the longer term.

The effects (benefits, counter-benefits, costs, and savings) accruing to different actors as a consequence of the generation and use of information, either informal or formalized in products and services, can be mapped. This involves a structured presentation of the short-, medium-, and long-term effects related to each category of user in the constituencies concerned in the development objective.

Some of the benefits that were mentioned in the previous chapter may be observed at the macro (national) level and in the long term. They may be easier to identify in this context in relation to problem areas or critical development issues. It is doubtful that short-term benefits could be observed on the macro scale; they should rather be sought in the area of long-term sociocultural changes, although an impact on global economic performance and internal and international competitiveness may be looked for in the short or medium term. An interesting question is whether fertilization of nonformal and nonconscious information by formal, solid information takes place so that the latter, and actions based upon it, becomes more appropriate for problem-solving. In answering this question, one should be careful not to impose a particular cultural bias; coherence, logic, and appropriateness can be judged only from within the community concerned or on the basis of a consensus among the various stakeholders.

Moving from the short term toward the long term presents the most difficulty. Perhaps a solution lies in being able to articulate a "nested hierarchy" of short-, mid-, and long-term goals. This exercise can be compared with that used in translating broad mission statements into broad goal statements, then broad objectives, and, finally, specific tasks.

Equality of access

Srinavasan (1977) provides an example of models that have emerged from development science. Speaking of measuring income distribution, he suggested that

> What one should be concerned with is equality of "access," be it to educational facilities, medical facilities, job opportunities, and not necessarily with equality of "success"... [because the latter approach] would not call for institutional change. [One should] measure the degree to which equality of "access" and fairness of the operation of the system is observed.

In measuring equality of access to opportunities, it is almost impossible not to also measure the information channels leading to educational facilities, medical facilities, job opportunities, or the development of the enterprises.

Global computer networking is changing the whole environment of the information field. It no longer consists of database searches and document delivery; it runs the whole gamut of formal and informal communications, which is undergoing historic changes. Although the volume of traffic on electronic networks like Internet is a good indicator of the density of information facilities, it can be a close surrogate of benefits in international comparisons when measured by type of transaction relative to GNP, population, and education levels. Timeliness, comprehensiveness, and reuse of information depend largely upon access to international data networks. Intracountry comparisons — between capital city and other urban and rural areas, central and peripheral parts of the country — can also be based on use of data networks. If the networks could provide figures about their subscribers or users broken down by socioprofessional category or about traffic by type (e-mail, access to databases, file transfer among branches of an organization), this would be another measure of access. Although this has not been done in many Third World countries, they will soon judge themselves and be judged in these terms. Lack of access to networks and databases is itself a measure of inequality, in an international context, because it prevents access to information and the chance to benefit from it.

Equality of access (or preferably equal opportunity of access) must also be considered in relation to its effectiveness for the worst-off segments of the population, such as handicapped people or geographically scattered rural populations. Appropriate information resources and telecommunication facilities made available to remote rural communities may contribute to improving their economic performance and well-being and, thus, to reducing internal migration. Equal opportunity of access should also alleviate physical barriers as well as sociocultural ones, like language. Another facet of information benefits may be their overall contribution to alleviating these barriers.

Appropriateness

One may contend that it is impossible for information to have intrinsic value. Its worth always depends on other factors, such as context, timeliness, availability of other information, usefulness, and applicability to specific needs. If, for example, a user receives a piece of information that he or she already knows, the message is useless, unless confirmation is needed. Also important is the background of the receiver. For example, the information that a patient's blood pressure is 190 over 150 is of no use to someone with no medical background, even if the patient may have a stroke because of this condition.

Although the absence of validity factors may jeopardize the use of information, it may not eliminate the value information has in itself, at least with regard to a collective use in the medium- or long-term. Even though most people will never go to the National Library and the information it holds is not appropriate for most of them, this does not imply that the information has no value.

One problem of libraries and information science services concerned with "information for development" is that a great deal of the information they contain is not relevant to the needs of their users. Neelameghan (1981) noted that "the use of information is also dependent upon the appropriateness of the information accessed. Therefore providing equal access to information to everyone does not ensure equal benefit to everyone." He lists dimensions along which the appropriateness of information might be assessed. They include appropriateness to the purpose; to users' characteristics; to the application environment; to the medium of information transfer; with respect to quality; with respect to time of availability; and with respect to the economics and cost of access and usability. He further stressed that

> Efficient and effective use of information in a system or country also depends on the level of development of the infrastructure; this may vary with the sectors within a country and among countries. Hence the differential benefit from information even if access is "equal" to everybody. Therefore, one benefit that should not be overlooked is an improvement in the appropriateness of information, which information systems may achieve in transforming and transferring both indigenous and exogenous information.

Benefits as seen by politicians

The challenge of getting decision-makers to focus on long-term benefits is difficult. Economists, who are key players in government and business decision-making, ask, with one voice, for quantitative data showing the returns on a proposed investment in information services.

However, returns on investment are not always evaluated in financial terms by politicians, but quite often in terms of their constituents' perceptions of the value. Roads and dams are seen to have great value because of the impact on the voting public. For politicians, benefits may be seen in terms of political advantage. If information has contributed to decisions that have resulted in increased employment opportunities, the politicians making the decisions are more likely to be re-elected.

In developing countries as elsewhere, the economic or technical rationale supporting a decision is likely to be revised, and possibly discarded, on the basis of a political rationale. Also, politicians are more likely to support projects that have demonstrable short-term benefits. A way must be found, for example, through cost–benefit analysis, to demonstrate the incremental benefits over the short, medium, and the long term, particularly within the context of specific policy objectives associated with particular governments. In this respect, it is worth considering information components as inseparable parts of "clusters of investments."

Although these issues should be given due consideration throughout the selection of benefits and elaboration of indicators, this project is not devoted to developing a catalogue of sales arguments for politicians in connection with information related projects. It must also provide the academic and professional communities with workable ideas and serve high-level decision-makers, who do pay attention to a wide range of factors.

As previously mentioned, any change in the current patterns of information provision and use is accompanied by a change in the balance of power. People in office may well perceive the latter as a cost that they would rather avoid. Therefore, it may be useful to analyze the power shifts likely to result from new information facilities, to be able to make explicit the costs and benefits to those in leadership positions.

Cost–benefit analysis

Cost–benefit analysis (CBA) is a systematic method for comparing alternative means of meeting specific objectives. The process can be broken down into eight steps:

- Establish and define the goals and objectives;
- Formulate appropriate assumptions;
- Identify alternatives for accomplishing the objectives;

- Determine the benefits and values, costs and burdens of each alternative;

- Evaluate alternatives by comparing their benefits and values with their costs and burdens;

- Test the sensitivity of the analysis to major uncertainties;

- Present the results; and

- Recommend the best means of meeting the objectives.

All decisions that involve spending money, and most do, weigh, more or less consciously, the costs (and burdens) and the benefits (and values) of one or more alternatives. The trick is identifying all potentially practical choices. Even if one can find only one new alternative, the status quo implicitly becomes the other (or old) choice and one must defend it or explain why it is untenable. Choosing to undertake one information project in a developing country over another, or to maintain the status quo, is also a cost–benefit decision.

If an information project is undertaken when only its benefits and values have been identified, weighted, and made explicit, then costs and burdens are implicitly inferred by the decision-makers regardless of whether the project designers and defenders intend them to do so. In an era of increasing economic pressures and costs, leaving costs and burdens in the implicit realm is less and less satisfactory (some might even say dangerous) because decision-makers are left in the dark as to what those costs may be. Consequently, they may grossly overestimate or underestimate the true costs over the project's duration in relation to the projected benefits. Two extreme outcomes are possible. Decision-makers may unwittingly approve a project in which the long-term costs far outweigh the benefits, because the costs were unknown. The other case is that they may unwittingly disapprove of a project in which the long-term benefits far outweigh the costs.

An "information project" contemplated in a developing country should propose a series of value enhancements to the five categories of tasks considered in the Knowledge Worker Productivity model: marginally productive activities, reading, analyzing, writing, and communicating (see under *Benefits for organizations* below), but probably using a more detailed list. For example, a new information resource, like an office automation network, might be expected to help decision-makers improve their drafting and revising capabilities; streamline, simplify, and mechanize formal and informal exchanges between offices; improve the speed and effectiveness of local and central information storage and retrieval systems; indexing; or primary and secondary distribution of data and documents; and so on.

Under a classic CBA approach, the project team would then be required to identify benefits, distinguishing between quantitative and qualitative benefits, and between recurring and nonrecurring benefits. Next, the proposal should identify costs, distinguishing between one-time and recurring, between fixed and variable, and between the traditional "object classes of cost," such as labour costs, material costs, and equipment costs. Based on this analysis, the project proposal should contain a list of illustrative benefits that would resemble a list of indicators (see indicators discussed below under *Benefits for organizations*).

In discussing the appropriateness of CBA, a number of points resulting from the underlying assumptions and methods used in CBA were highlighted as commonly cited limitations:

1. Benefits and costs should be measured in terms of willingness to pay.

2. Various types of benefits and costs can be aggregated and expressed quantitatively using a common numerical value.

3. Costs and benefits can then be measured and compared through this common numerical value.

4. The distribution effect of policy choices is put aside.

5. All "real" benefits and costs must be taken into account without regard to the reasons people have for viewing something as a cost or a benefit.

6. The same priorities and ranking of values should apply across different social contexts, without regard to the contexts (for

example, whether people's choices are voluntary or autono-
mous, or reflect a particular distribution of power).

7. All relevant moral and political considerations must be fitted
into the pre-established benefit and cost formula.

8. People's values and understanding about what is reasonable
must be fitted into a utility formula treating risks and uncertainties as statistical variables.

9. A benefit or cost in one domain is equally a benefit or cost in
some other domain.

10. All benefits are measured against all the costs.

11. The benefits and costs considered are those to the producer and
the investor, but not necessarily to the user; the cost of using
information and information systems is often not taken into
account.

12. Benefits are defined as favourable comparisons of the costs and
benefits of two alternatives, while costs are unfavourable comparisons. Thus a benefit at one level can in fact be considered a
cost at another level, a benefit to one person can be a cost to
another, and a cost for one alternative can be a benefit relative
to another.

Most critics of CBA focus on the first four points listed above. The
cultural criticisms are directed at points 6 to 8 and, secondarily,
points 2 and 4.

In CBA, it is imperative to state the assumptions and terms of
reference from the outset so that everyone examining the data for
accuracy and completeness is in a position to know the full benefits
and the full costs including those in the near term and far term, sunk
costs (those which cannot be recovered), and what economists sometimes call displaced benefits and costs or "externalities." The distinction between fixed and variable costs is also useful, particularly if
charges are to be imposed. It is difficult to decide at what level costs
should be assigned. Also, the allocation of costs associated with
administrative and overhead, for example, can be complex.

Decision-makers may not only infer costs associated with each
alternative, they will also have to guess the relative costs, which are

much harder to determine because they are the result of comparing both alternative costs and benefits. Rarely are before-and-after studies conducted, so the decisions are never validated.

CBA provides for differentiation between quantifiable and non-quantifiable benefits and costs and distinction between efficiency and effectiveness factors. Too often, critics unjustifiably assume that using CBA requires that all benefits and costs be quantified and made tangible.

The CBA approach does take "social norms" into account. Many factors should be considered when selecting the preferred alternative. The less-quantifiable ones may be overriding and mitigate against a "straight economic solution." Every decision made by a government to proceed with a project is a political decision. However, often decision-makers who override the CBA recommendations on social or political grounds do not have the courage to state their assumptions and premises because they fear they will be accused of wasting taxpayers' money.

CBA is not a panacea. The decision-makers must make the final decision, not the CBA. Final decisions must take into account not only economic factors, but the political as well as the social and humanitarian benefits and costs. Information has values and benefits that transcend the purely economic dimension.

In applying the CBA approach to projects of all kinds, decision-makers do not adequately consider the substantial differences between information projects and noninformation projects, like building a dam or a bridge. As a result, the discount rates they use to calculate the so-called "benefit stream" and "cost stream" are weighted in favour of the short term because the officials do not seem to understand that the benefits of many information projects take much longer to accrue. The short-term benefits of information projects tend to be in terms of consciousness raising; mid- and long-term benefits (the "payout period" to use CBA jargon) are not evident until much later than those resulting from a bridge or a dam. If decision-makers can be persuaded to use a lower discount rate in the CBA calculations for information projects, then the chances of successfully demonstrating the return on investment for such projects are better. Perhaps another factor to associate with any identified benefit is lead time for its materialization.

Participants suggested that some sort of generalized CBA framework might be developed, using a concrete example, to provide guidance in applying CBA methods in other cases.

Applicability of CBA to information projects in developing countries

Comparing Maslow's hierarchy of needs with a similar set of information needs (Horton 1983) may help in identifying the kinds of projects or situations in which CBA may not be appropriate. At the bottom of the hierarchy is the need for coping information, followed by helping, educating, enlightening, and edifying information. The model may be used without necessarily retaining its notion of hierarchy, which is not exempt from a cultural bias. Assuming that the needs at the lower level are met up to the minimum required for sustaining life, many people will seek information at the top level; the need for dignity is no less important to starving people.

In general, the closer one is to the bottom of the hierarchy (trying to establish and use information resources to cope with day-to-day challenges like securing enough food, shelter, and health care), the more difficult it becomes to use a CBA framework to explain, defend, and justify expenditures for information projects. This may be because it is so difficult to put a value on human life or, less dramatically, to put a price tag on the fundamental resources needed to sustain and nourish human beings.

As one moves up the hierarchy and reaches the levels of education and enlightenment (which presumes that the lower order needs have been minimally met), it becomes progressively easier to justify CBA approaches to decisions about supporting information projects (the benefits, which are more tangible and quantifiable rather than subjective and moral, can be articulated with greater precision and outweigh the costs).

It is perplexing that the need for coping information, which is so urgent in developing countries, is the most difficult to justify using the CBA approach. It might be useful to correlate Maslow's hierarchy with a set of information needs for a developing country rather than an individual. Such a list might include information for production of food (agriculture), information for safety (health), and so forth, and might be more responsive to a CBA approach.

Notwithstanding the difficult and complex problems confronting investors, sponsors, and information project managers, the project team should make an effort to use CBA analysis, even for the "lower order" types of projects. In these days of recession, policy-makers and decision-makers are scrutinizing competing project proposals carefully. Those who are explaining, defending, and justifying information projects must use every strategy and tactic at their disposal to ensure success.

A response to the apparent difficulty of using CBA in developing-country contexts might be found in developing some hypothetical policies that governments could follow in deciding how much to charge users, depending on the kind of information resource involved, and comparing them with normal commercial practice in the private sector (Horton 1984), as shown in Table 2.

Coping information may be provided by hotline telephone services dealing with emergency matters of health, safety, and security (like police, fire, first aid, and ambulance); helping information by government enquiry services, agencies, community groups, and

Table 2. Policies for the provision of various levels of information by the public or private sector.

Type of information	Proposed public-sector price	Private-sector price
Coping	Free	Less than fully competitive and possibly subsidized
Helping	Less than full cost recovery	Competitive
Enlightening	Full cost recovery	Fully competitive
Enriching	Less than fully competitive	Fully competitive market pricing
Edifying	Fully competitive	Fully competitive

corporations; enlightening information by community and neighbourhood information centres; enriching information by professional services; and edifying information by information analysis centres.

CBA policies that a government might adopt in helping it decide whether to approve an information project in the context of a free market economy are listed below. Arguments will arise as to whether a particular information project should be classified as primarily related to coping, helping, or other type of information need. However, information available and used at any one level may have secondary effects at one or several other levels. This versatility of information is indeed a major difficulty in the assessment of benefits. Disagreement is normal, and governments can deal with it on a peer review basis (using a panel of experts).

The criteria upon which the acceptance of projects in the various categories might be justified can be outlined as follows:

- Coping information: Expected benefits do not equal aggregate costs; nonquantifiable benefits substantially exceed quantifiable benefits; quantifiable benefits are impossible or extremely difficult to assess; no amortization or period for return on investment is specified; no discount rate is specified.

- Helping information: Expected benefits approximate or equal aggregate costs, or are no less than a specified percentage of costs; nonquantifiable benefits are approximately equal to quantifiable benefits; quantifiable benefits are difficult but not impossible to assess, or at least estimate; amortization or return on investment period is extended; discount rate is reduced.

- Enlightening information: Expected benefits are at least equal to, but may exceed aggregate costs; quantifiable benefits exceed nonquantifiable benefits and can be measured in a relatively straightforward manner; amortization or return on investment period is within conventional norms; discount rate is within conventional norms.

- Enriching information: Expected benefits clearly exceed aggregate costs; the return on investment approaches or equals the current estimated government rate for its capital and other noninformation projects; quantifiable benefits significantly exceed nonquantifiable benefits and are easily measured; amortization period and discount rate within the current government specification for capital and other noninformation projects or, at least, within conventional norms.

- Edifying information: Expected benefits substantially exceed aggregate costs; the return on investment exceeds the current established government norm for capital and other noninformation projects by a significant amount; few, if any nonquantifiable benefits are present; amortization or return on investment period and discount rate are well within generally accepted government norms.

The Common Pool Resources model

The possibility of using an alternative model of CBA that allows for an investigation of the creation and use of information systems for development as a form of collective behaviour rather than individual behaviour was considered. Ostrom's (1990) Common Pool Resources (CPR) model was thought to offer a potential advantage, when used in appropriate situations. This is a CBA model that accounts for the influence of group norms on an individual's decision to change the status quo — a critical factor for success that is not accounted for in "classic" CBA models.

Considering an information resource within a CPR approach, the resource system, also referred to as the stock, consists of the index language and grammar that affect the flow of resource units. The resource units consist of citations, texts, formulae, and other information that are appropriated from the resource system. The stakeholders are appropriators (recognized participants and users), providers (who arrange for the provisions necessary to create the CPR), and producers (who assess the need for, design, and construct the CPR). Some people may participate in the information CPR in one or more of these roles. In the established approach to information systems, owners, operators, and users are considered, and possibly view each other, as separate if not antagonist players. One advantage of the CPR model may be to reconcile them.

In the benefit–cost–norms–discount analysis, benefits are considered to be what appropriators expect to gain from the information system; costs are what appropriators expect to invest in the system; norms are the behaviours shared by appropriators that reflect the value they place on the rules of governance of the information system; discount rate is the value that an individual appropriator places on the stock (index language and grammar) through which resource units are retrieved from the information system. The discount rate is determined by the appropriator in terms of immediate and future benefits expected from the appropriation of resource units.

Ostrom bases her model on the decisions that must be made by people (potential appropriators, providers, and producers of a CPR information system) in considering how they can organize themselves, based on their shared norms, by developing rules and strategies to govern their interaction within the information CPR to avoid overcrowding, overuse, and short-term discount rates and to enhance long-term sustainability of the CPR. Appropriators base their support of the CPR on their short-term experience, long-term expectations of benefits, and their willingness to pay the costs of maintenance of the CPR as long as benefits meet their expectations and their cost of participating in the CPR is reasonable compared with the costs born by the other appropriators.

By including consideration of norms and discount rates, general predictions about the appropriators' needs for and likely success in sustaining a CPR-type information system can be made. On this basis, an information CPR can be designed in cooperation with appropriators. The design should reflect their past behaviour and enhance their future ability to map information from their native system to the information CPR. The mapping of a known system to a new one can combine the power of both while assuring individual appropriators that old positions of influence in creating and controlling information will not be entirely lost. It decreases the need for appropriators to adopt entirely new ways of making meaning from information, and allows for norms of social behaviour to be transferred from the native to the new system.

Benefits for organizations

The assessment of benefits for organizations should be undertaken in the framework of an Organization Resource Management (ORM) model. The assumptions in an ORM model are that

- The concept of information resources encompasses information services, systems, sources, human resources, and facilities (similar to the concept of information infrastructure);

- Information should be regarded as a full-fledged factor of production; and

- All factors of production should be managed with four objectives in mind: maximize value gained from using a factor, minimize cost involved in using a factor, assign accountability for the use of a factor, and ensure continuous supply of a factor.

In the context of developing countries, minimizing the cost of using a factor may be complemented by two further objectives: minimize effort in using a factor and minimize the risk of unwanted external influences (in particular, abuse of power).

The ORM model should take into account the specificity of the sectors, sociocultural factors affecting the organization and individual people, the various kinds of organizations (such as foreign firms, public or private organizations, large organizations, and medium and small enterprises). It is questionable whether the ORM model could also be applied in the case of individual entrepreneurs and semiformal groups.

Benefits can be traced on the basis of the Knowledge Worker Productivity model, several adaptations of which have been developed from the original version produced by Booz, Allen, and Hamilton. It divides information or knowledge work into five categories: marginally productive activities, reading, analyzing, writing, and communicating.

However, this model is more concerned with the role of information producer than information user. Marginally productive activities include information seeking and organizing information. Because these activities are essential, it would be better to consider them as separate categories. The model would require extensive revision to reflect key functions better and, more importantly, to apply it to nonformal communications or those based on oral tradition. Also, users' costs are a key factor in the assessment of costs and benefits.

Short-term internal benefits for organizations may take the form of improved productivity (efficiency); higher quality decision-making; timely recognition of opportunities and threats; improved performance of tasks (effectiveness); less time needed to implement tasks; improved learning curve (faster, sharper incline); increased importance of work function; discontinuation or replacement of certain manual tasks by automated ones (in cases where this corresponds to a true increase in effectiveness); greater interchangeability of personnel; elimination of intermediate processing steps; greater task integration; improved synchronization of tasks; less need for clerical support; less reliance on paper files; greater reuse of information assets; more sharing of information assets; faster response time; reduced turnaround time; tighter security and fewer violations of information confidentiality or privacy; less lost or missing information.

Avoiding duplication might also be seen as a benefit, although some duplication may be beneficial. Another possible benefit is avoiding obsolescence of the work force, at least in competitive environments; a rate of decay in work force capability can perhaps be derived from the obsolescence of literature in the related fields. Similarly, one might try to assess the contribution of libraries to literacy and its downstream socioeconomic benefits using an estimate of a decay rate in literacy rates in the absence of proper provision of reading material. In the public sector, productivity gains may be regarded as a potential benefit of paramount importance.

Gains in productivity seem to occur more often when people are excluded from the processes of operational use of information (such as in computer-assisted manufacturing or the use of robots in manufacturing). In the service sector, productivity is lower and more related to the number of transactions than their effectiveness.

A tentative list of benefit indicators for a computer-based information system in a government agency, regardless of program or subject field, was proposed; it may well apply to any other type of formal organization. It covers a number of specific areas:

- Overall accountability and management,
- Security, integrity, and reliability,
- Interconnectedness and integration of operations,
- Quality of data and information in the system,
- Productivity in the organization,
- Improvements in organizational effectiveness, and
- Improvements in information management.

Participants in the computer conference discussed benefit assessment with reference to a hypothetical rural community resource centre. The results are presented in Appendix 3.

Chapter 4

INDICATORS AND ASSESSMENT METHODS

———————■———————

Characteristics of indicators

In selecting indicators, consideration should be given to the following points:

- Data collection and analysis should be as simple as possible;

- Interpretation of the indicators should be straightforward;

- The indicators should point to benefits that are usually given attention by policy- and decision-makers; and

- The indicators should lead to straightforward conclusions, which should be intelligible, if not attractive, to those who are going to act upon them.

It would be helpful to identify each proposed benefit and indicator according to its intended target user. At least two categories of users should be considered: policymakers (general level) and technical decision-makers (operational level). Including scholars in the latter group or forming a third one should also be considered.

Contrary to popular belief, most decision-makers in developing countries, and the population at large, understand the importance of accessing and managing information and knowledge. However, communities and people have their own values and immediate interests, conscious or otherwise, with regard to information. Any potential indicator should be checked against these.

Indicators should be defined and grouped according to the three main purposes for which they may be used:

- To evaluate performance in relation to a set of objectives, depending on the specific area of endeavour or project;

- To guide the planning of services or activities where indicators are needed as a reference point to guide the process; and

- To support a proposal where one has to take into account the situation and needs of the relevant decision-maker (or group of decision-makers with different interests).

Any potential indicator will likely fit into one of these categories; if not, additional categories could be considered.

Four types of indicators, based on input cost, output, effectiveness, and domain (see, for example, Griffiths and King 1993), could be considered in relation to information impact on development:

- Operational performance indicators, which relate to output (such as productivity, efficiency, cost per output, cost by attribute level, and productivity by attribute level);

- Effectiveness indicators, which relate output to use (such as user satisfaction, turnover rate, amount of use by attribute level, satisfaction by attribute level, and amount of use by satisfaction level);

- Cost-effectiveness indicators, which relate input to use ratios (such as cost per use, cost per user, cost per capita, and cost by satisfaction level); and

- Impact indicators, which relate actual to potential use (such as market penetration, uses per capita, and needs fill rate).

Some of these indicators seem to relate more to information systems, but could be adapted to evaluate the impact of information use. For example, timeliness of service prevents delays in reacting to a given challenge or problem. Cost effectiveness and impact indicators seem more appropriate, but might have to be made more explicit.

Assessments must consider all significant issues; they should not be restricted to what is easy to measure. In particular, indicators should not overlook the informal information processes and resources or the qualitative aspects of user satisfaction.

To prepare a consistent series of indicators of long-, medium-, and short-term potential benefits, one should produce a nested hierarchy based on broad mission statement, broad goals, broad objectives, and specific tasks. Focusing on the short term or on narrow constituencies for the sake of greater visibility may restrict assessment to information systems themselves rather than their impact on development.

Two methods for analyzing the links between information and development goals and intermediate objectives can be contemplated. The first is correlation or regression analysis (see Hayes and Erickson 1982) where the dependent variables are indicators of goal achievement (like statistics on health status) and independent variables are size of the health-care labour force, for example, and information capability. Second, surveys may be directed at intermediate-level contributors to health care to determine the extent of their use of information and the consequences of that use in terms of health care. The second method is more practical because of the better quality of data on dependent and independent variables for regression analysis that it may produce. Statistical analysis based upon readily available aggregate data is often unproductive. It is important to collect meaningful data that relate as closely as possible to the type of information studied and its role.

General indicators may be a combination of sector-related indicators. However, the latter are context dependent and, thus, a large number of cases must be reviewed before one can consolidate them and produce meaningful aggregates.

In principle, indicators should have several formal properties. They should be mutually compatible and they should be relative measurements (ratios or indexes), such as the number of potential users as a proportion of the number of actual users. This simplifies comparisons with other measures, among various types of information provision systems, and among different situations in relation to a particular mode of access or service.

An indicator may be defined on a conceptual level (abstract domain) and on an empirical level (physical domain). For example, regarding the immediate benefit to an extension worker using a rural community resource centre identified as "increased knowledge (or reduced uncertainty) about the community's demand for information," at the conceptual level, the indicator might be demand for information expressed by the community. At the empirical level it might be average number of records in the reference section of the centre during the first semester or percentage of records, classified by information content (an ad hoc classification scheme should be attached) detected in the reference section of the centre during the first semester. There can be more than one conceptual definition per benefit and more than one empirical definition per conceptual definition. Both conceptual and empirical definitions must be stated clearly so that a third party can assess their quality and pertinence.

Regarding information projects, a distinction ought to be made between indicators related to the status or capacity of the information activities (such as number of professionals, articles published, and number of information unit services) and specific indicators related to the convenience or feasibility of developing a project and the results of such a project, which can involve cost reduction, improved services, wider coverage, and other aspects. The aim of the indicator is different in these two cases. Taking this into account may make it easier to define the most appropriate indicator.

Describing constituencies

Most studies of the provision and use of information in developing countries offer only a limited overview of the environment. They tend to overlook the roles and functions in the communication cycle that are not directly associated with the studied activity or service. Attention is seldom paid to other mechanisms by which the main user groups receive information, especially the informal channels. Researchers often use methods and a reference framework that are peculiar to each study. Their results can, thus, not be compared or combined.

Once a constituency or a segment of one has been selected for an investigation of the impact of information, basic data are needed about the population to allow adequate interpretation of observations. Data elements or descriptive parameters were tentatively identified and organized in Taylor's (1991) model of an "information use environment" (IUE). This model was somewhat revised and expanded as a result of the computer conference and seven sets of background data were identified:

- **People**: demographic data (age, sex, marital status, race, and level of education), occupational data (profession and position), sociological data (income level, personal networks, status in and interaction with the community, and media use).

- **Setting**: location, size of the organization, domain(s) of interest, culture of the organization, and history.

- **Culture**: attitudes toward education, new technology, risk taking, innovation, information, knowledge, and source of authority.

- **Problems**: sets of perceived priorities, dynamics of those problems, nature of the problems, such as well-structured or ill-structured, simple or complex, familiar or new, agreed upon or not agreed upon.

- **Expected solutions to the problems**: for a given set of people, what constitutes resolution of a typical problem, what role does information play in resolving the problem, and which information could contribute to which aspect of the solution.

- **Process of problem-solving and decision-making**: where does the impetus come from, what are the recognized formal steps and factors, and what are the nonformal or "nonrational" factors involved.

- **Available information sources**: mapping of all formal and informal sources and access channels known by the population and available to it.

Describing the constituency need not be a profound anthropological study, but it should be a sufficiently precise description of the social machinery to provide guidance in interpreting the data that will be gathered on the use of and benefits from information. A suitable presentation of the IUE goes beyond the rather superficial descriptions of user group that one usually finds.

The model for an IUE summarized above must be tested and consolidated; the sets of data must be validated. A series of IUEs for the principal constituencies in developing countries must be devised. Then the appropriate data can be collected with a view to documenting the parameters and outlining suitable data-gathering methods. The model might then be revised if necessary.

The IUE model could then be applied in a variety of settings in a cooperative effort to assemble a series of IUEs covering as many types of constituencies as possible in a range of developing countries. The various sets of parameters could be the focus of particular studies. If their implementation is guided by common concepts and methods, such studies might facilitate the progressive building of IUEs. The descriptive parameters contemplated in the IUEs should be distinguished from the indicators of the impact of information, which are intended to focus on information benefits only.

The whole communication cycle, from generation to assimilation, has not been studied in specific institutions or communities of developing countries. Comprehensive description of its structure and operation, taking due account of such factors as maintenance of equipment, provision of supplies, and effectiveness of mail, for example, and encompassing formal and informal channels, may be a requisite for understanding information flows and, later, for explaining the perception of benefits resulting from information.

Unconscious values, emotions, and "nonrational" perceptions of information seem to affect behaviour in using information, especially information from formal sources. Social psychology studies might prove most helpful in providing insight into these phenomena.

It would also be worthwhile to assess the difference in richness and composition of the information environment of comparable groups operating in the formal and informal economy. One might assume that a harder struggle for survival and greater autonomy among those in the informal sector have resulted in an original and possibly richer information base. Should this hypothesis be verified, it might help in the identification of parameters that are meaningful for describing IUEs as well as in the design of alternative strategies. The investigation could be attempted by mapping memorized sources of information as discussed in Appendix 3 and below.

Building impact assessment into information projects

Projects involved in providing information — to rural communities, in higher education as a tool for planning, for health services, to politicians, for building plans, and other uses — must be analyzed to see what makes them valuable generally. One common factor is that these uses are all related to a specific need.

Information, in the abstract, means little to the engineer, the agriculturist, the farmer, the craftsman, or the doctor. Information must be subject oriented, or otherwise delimited, to be relevant for specific groups. Considering information for information's sake is a dead end. The future in this field seems to lie in specific, well-conceived projects undertaken in association with specialist groups, or groups with a broad common interest.

Seminars or workshops should be organized with two target groups: workers specializing in a subject or activity; and the top managers in the same subject or activity. The seminars would take place during the implementation of projects for the development of information services, at regular intervals from the design stage to the final evaluation, to identify and possibly measure the benefits. Only when a series of such projects has been completed will we be able to formulate a comprehensive series of adequate assessment indicators.

In information research, funding bodies often want "quick and dirty" results; thus, no consideration has been given to the question now being raised: How do the various professions view information?

Simple information support projects, whose variables can be easily controlled, could be designed specifically to measure benefits and costs while information is actually being delivered. Such projects should include a precisely identified series of value enhancements to the various categories of work in the Knowledge Workers Productivity model or to the roles and functions of the communication cycle. By using a CBA framework, the projects should distinguish between qualitative and quantitative benefits, recurring and nonrecurring ones, and also distinguish between one time and recurring costs, fixed and variable costs, and the object of costs. A sufficient timespan should be allowed for the projects to produce observable effects. Information use and its impact should be evaluated at regular intervals during implementation and several years after the completion of the projects.

The formulation of information-related projects is often carried out within a short time, possibly on the basis of pre-established models. This does not allow for the gathering of the data needed to gain an adequate understanding of the IUE and the initial situation. Preproject or initial phases should be introduced to obtain such information and data about current information flow and uses and their associated costs.

The benefit indicators used by the United States' General Accounting Office when assessing information activities were discussed as an example of a framework for investigating benefits from information projects (see Appendix 4). They may also apply in studies of information in organizations as discussed below.

The assessment of benefits requires a thorough knowledge of the current needs for providing information. A series of surveys or market studies was proposed to provide a comprehensive picture of information needs, the response provided by new or enhanced information services, and user satisfaction. It should determine

- Users' attitudes toward the information services before and after the introduction of the enhancement;

- Information resources, by systematic survey (infomapping) in a selected group of institutions or sectors;

- Information needs for selected sectors or groups of institutions;

- Response of newly established centres or services to the identified needs;

- Increase in information delivery and use;

- Requirements for databases in selected sectors;

- Coverage, and whether it matches the identified needs and use of databases;

- Information packaging needs;

- Proportion of incorrect responses;

- Database and information services users;

- Computerized and traditional management systems;

- Data transmission facilities and traffic;

- Use of telecommunication facilities;

- Information manpower resources;

- Information training facilities (with evaluation);

- Information standards requirements; and

- Cooperation protocols among information producers and providers.

There is no list of all the information-related projects that have been carried out in developing countries. We hope that research might be undertaken to fill this gap. However, it seems that more attention has been paid to building information infrastructure, especially at the national level, than to providing information services. It would be interesting to investigate the rationale, costs, benefits, and outcomes of the respective approaches with a view to suggesting an appropriate balance between them.

Assessing information benefits for organizations

Analytical and quantitative methods for assessing value in organizations are increasingly used and have significantly contributed to the understanding of information activities. However, they may be time consuming, costly, and not accurate enough. Current deficiencies in the theoretical foundations and their empirical verification in information science create further problems in the design and implementation of CBA. Regular procedures for the overall assessment of organizations and auditing may also be unnatural in the environment we are considering.

Assuming that information is recognized as a production factor, one might produce input–output matrices of the various production factors to identify potential benefits systematically. Indicators can be developed to trace the long-term benefits resulting from a richer information environment made possible by information-related investments and short- or medium-term benefits resulting from the empowerment of the organization, its staff, and management.

Information impact and indicators must be defined that easily relate to critical managerial needs, such as the ability to cope with turbulence, rapid change, and uncertainties, and track greater effectiveness as a result of better knowledge and use of information resources. The critical incident method may offer a suitable framework for such investigations.

A decay rate for workforce skills may be derived from those reported in related areas. On this basis, the amount of information support needed by the professional staff to keep their knowledge base up-to-date can be estimated. Assuming that a large proportion of the decay would be better offset through continuing education, only a fraction of the decay rate would be allocated to information support. The ratio is to be applied to the annual payroll of the considered staff. For example, a decay rate of 10 years would thus call for 10% of the payroll per year, of which 2 or 3% would be for information support. The reality of the decay as well as the effect of such as effort could be assessed by looking at the comprehensiveness, relevance, and timeliness of the information used by the professional staff as reflected in its document production.

Time savings can be assessed by measuring time required to obtain access to correct information from the information resources at various times during the process of strengthening the available information support.

Reduction of duplication might be examined by reviewing the annual reports and interviewing the executives of a representative set of organizations in a given sector. It would be necessary to find out what duplicate activities took place because staff were unaware of duplication or were aware but carried them out for various reasons, and what activities were rejected on the basis of available information.

Studies of the correlation between investment and recurrent spendings in the production of information and research could also be considered, although research outputs in developing countries are often nonformal (for example, contributions to extension programs and advisory services).

Programs geared toward computerization of information- and communication-intensive processes, which are receiving increasing attention, may be appropriate for impact assessments. These are hybrid applications of information technology with clear strategic implications concerning, for instance, the modernization of the financial sector, customs and tax computerization, or management of public expenditures and debt.

Assessing the impact of information on specific constituencies

The mapping of IUEs should serve as the starting point in identifying critical issues, which might then be linked, if appropriate, with broader development priorities, such as improved sanitation and participation of intermediate groups.

There are many facets to specific development issues. For example, was it the discovery of a vaccine against polio, the infrastructure to distribute and administer it, information about its benefits, or a combination of these that led to the virtual eradication of this disease in many countries? The problem lies in trying to separate the components and measure the benefits derived from each. There are three possible solutions to this problem:

- Use a nested hierarchy, in which the final product and its benefits (such as eradication of a disease) are disaggregated into a series of successive required inputs.

- Consider which of the lower-level inputs are information dependent and to what extent (in the polio vaccine, for example) a health-care plan, public awareness, personnel, and the vaccine are primarily information dependent; and logistics, like transportation and supplies, are not. Each of these factors, or critical resources, can be further broken down to a point where information inputs can be more clearly specified and assessed.

- Measure the value of the benefits directly related to information by, for example, considering the percentage distribution of the cost of the various factors and applying it to the value of the ultimate result, when such a result is more or less defined. With regard to health programs, even though calculations might be suspect, public health officials often quote a "cost" of a particular disease.

Objective measurement at any level is not straightforward. It is difficult to obtain indicators of utility on a consistent scale that lead to objective interpretation. Subjective estimates by experts in the appropriate field may be a suitable alternative.

Assuming that the sources of information that are known and remembered are likely to be the ones that are beneficial, a preliminary overview can be gained by measuring, at successive intervals, the breadth and depth of formal and nonformal information that a sample of the population has memorized and used, or the "memorized directory" of information sources used in specific decision-making or problem-solving situations by the constituency.

Assessing the information richness of the environment

Qualitative and quantitative improvements in the formal information resources can be assessed using the following criteria:

- Enhancement of the infrastructure can be measured by calculating rate of coverage of the needs identified through market studies and the rate of use of computer and telecommunications facilities.

- Availability of information can be calculated from the coverage of the various sectors by databases and an index of the diversification of information products.

- The reliability of information can be measured by determining the rate of correct responses from, for example, a regular panel survey.

- The use of information can be assessed from both the number of users of centres and services and the diversity of the user groups.

- Impact on management could be measured by the number of organizations with well-defined general and information-management structures and procedures.

- Information-sharing can be observed from the number of online links, the number of networks, their scope, and coverage of the various sectors.

- Labour development can be assessed from the number of staff with information responsibilities and number of information-related courses.

- Cooperation may be reflected by the number of joint projects, joint committees, and active protocols for cooperation.

- Standardization can be traced by the number of information standards introduced and adopted over time.

As already stressed, one other facet of benefits of using information may be its eventual contribution to lowering the barriers to information, such as language, literacy, distance from sources, disabilities, and lack of financial resources.

The ingredients of a formula to measure equality of access to information include time, effort, cost, and distance in relation to income group or any other socioprofessional characteristic. Indicators to consider in assessing equality of access to data networks and telecommunications facilities at large, both within and among countries, are number of facilities available, total traffic, traffic per type of service, and cost in relation to basic country indicators or basic parameters specifying the considered socioprofessional groups.

Some direct measure of the cost of access can be made assuming that, in the absence of the information systems, each user would have to bear costs individually (the unit cost of acquisition and processing, plus overhead, would have to be multiplied by the number of users).

One would probably have to rely upon market surveys, through standing panels, for example, to assess the appropriateness of both formal and informal channels once the mapping of IUEs has provided enough background information for their design. The methods used by the European Economic Community's Information Market Observatory may provide a useful example in this area.

Using anecdotes

Systematically collecting a large number of examples, or anecdotes, about the use of information and its effect on problem-solving within specific and well-defined IUEs is an important and promising approach. Social studies of the use of information suffer from a lack of continuity and systematization. If a large enough series of well-structured cases is available, the co-occurrence of appropriate provision of information and effective resolution of problems could be established. In addition, the nature of the role of information and conditions for its use may be elucidated. This may provide a sufficient starting point for establishing causality.

Due attention must be paid to the fact that information uses and value are related to many diverse factors. The field of information lacks a set of common principles like the ones available in law and history, for example, to allow it to derive knowledge from anecdotes. For the anecdotes to be intelligible, not only should the IUEs be well defined, but the parameters revealed in the anecdotes should also be categorized according to the characteristics of the respective constituencies (cultural, socioeconomic, group size, scale of operation).

In the area of health-care improvement, for example, a considerable body of historical evidence, based on the work of the Pan American Health Organization and the World Health Organization, might indicate the impact of information on development, specifically in relation to the control, reduction, or elimination of certain diseases in developing countries. This historical approach might lead to further evidence documented by aid agencies working in other areas in developing countries, even though they may not have undertaken an assessment of the role of information outside the extension services.

It is probably possible, although by no means easy, to find examples of the value and usefulness of information (situations in which having the right information has made a difference). Sector professionals may prove a better source for examples than information professionals, who often do not see the end result of the supply of information. A post-mortem approach could also be tried, identifying the components of information or knowledge use in the development activities considered by developing countries to have been successful or disastrous (for example, see Horton and Lewis 1991).

Definition of the nature, topic, and scope of anecdotes must be determined on the basis of the perceptions of the concerned constituencies rather than on those of information specialists. Several methods could be used to collect the data, including Grounded Theory,

Priority and Performance Evaluation, and Critical Success Factors (for example, see Broadbent 1992; Davenport 1992).

Before evaluating a body of anecdotes, they must be categorized according to who collected what, when, and where, and to which IUEs and problem areas they are related. Second, some elements must be used to determine the reliability and credibility of the reporter. Third, one must decide whether the anecdotes make sense in the considered contexts and in relation to the problem being examined. Fourth, links must be established between the anecdotes and existing evidence: are they new, confirming, expanding, or contradicting it. Standard scales should be used in this validation process and it should be undertaken by individual judges or panels of specialists, who are familiar with the context and will not impose an external "common-sense" interpretation.

Assuming the anecdotes are properly calibrated, some statistical analysis can be attempted to extract a common set of variables; this will identify those that are relevant and their relation can be analyzed. In particular, such anecdotes can be measured by the critical incident method, which might provide some support to previous hypotheses on the impact of each of the variables. This approach might be limited to the extent that it does not offer evidence of causality and the variables would be limited by what is reported. However, it can give an indication of the effect of the various factors and a basis for designing further studies.

Assessing information impact through the market

Forcing users to pay for information may be the most straightforward way of assessing its use. Demand can be assumed to reflect utility. Market studies may be the best method, at least in the formal sector, to determine which types of information are regarded as the most useful and how much people would be prepared to pay for them. Such market studies could readily be undertaken with particular regard to the professional or practical usefulness of information in the mass media, the scope and amount of additional information required, and the price users would be ready to pay for this additional information.

To obtain market validation of benefits and check the likelihood of deriving benefits from the establishment of information industries, information projects should escape the quasi-exclusivity currently given to the government sector. Often, no significant attempt is made in the government sector to include cost-recovery mechanisms, which may allow it to become at least partly self-sustaining. More projects should be geared toward the private sector with the aim of trading information as a commodity. Such projects should be long term and start by building up the basic facilities, progressively shift support from the offer side to the demand side, then reduce support for demand until a state of self-sufficiency is reached (over about 10 years). They might take the form of low-risk, noncapital-intensive joint ventures to establish information enterprises, or even companies, from which economic demand could be monitored and, through it, socioeconomic benefits assessed.

Chapter 5

THE POST-CONFERENCE WORKSHOP

————■————

Objectives

The post-conference workshop was distinct from the computer conference, even though it was directly linked with it. Guided by the summary report of the computer conference and other documents resulting from it, workshop participants discussed ways in which the ideas explored during the conference could be used as the basis for practical approaches to assessing the impact of information on development. The workshop was not intended as a forum for detailed discussion, or approval, of the report of the computer conference. However, it was necessary to consider the validity of the conclusions reached so far.

The main objective of the workshop was to define criteria for the identification of indicators and to translate the conclusions of the computer conference into practical proposals for field-testing in developing countries, which will take place during the next phase of the effort. Participants were further encouraged to comment on the theme of the project and suggest areas for further investigation and follow-up activities.

Participants

To ensure maximum interaction and intensive group work, the number of participants was limited to 15. These participants, who were selected by IDRC (see Appendix 1), included five people who had also taken part in the computer conference (including the moderator). They provided continuity, but were not expected to defend or justify their contribution to the conference or its conclusions. Rather they would take a fresh look at the issues along with other professionals. Seven senior professionals, all but one from developing countries and all but one with a broad experience in the planning and management of information systems, also attended along with two IDRC program officers and a consultant, who was invited to serve as facilitator.

Schedule and organization

In a plenary session on the first day, participants were asked to describe their own background and their expectations from the workshop. The computer conference and its results were outlined, followed by a discussion of the goals, expected outcome, and assumptions of the workshop. A second session was devoted to organization of the working groups. Two groups of six participants each were set up with Kingo Mchombu and Wilson O. Aiyepeku as chairpersons and Forest Woody Horton, Jr and José-Marie Griffiths as rapporteurs for groups 1 and 2, respectively.

To help participants focus on practical problems, three case studies derived from IDRC project proposals were supplied. Both working groups were to consider "Information for decision-making in the Caribbean Community." The other two proposals — "Integrated information system for Thailand's rural development program" and "Capacity-building in electronic communications for development in Africa" — would each be dealt with by one of the groups, as a means of cross-checking its findings against the first case. The three projects were reviewed in some detail, with respect to their objectives, the critical success factors for each, their political, economic, and social environments, and other aspects to ensure that all participants had a fair understanding of the relevant details.

The following guidelines for the working groups were to be interpreted loosely:

- Both groups should examine the Caribbean case study in depth;

- Group 1 should also look at the Thailand project while group 2 studies the Africa project;

- Rapporteurs should "capture the essence" of each group's deliberations and report highlights in a plenary session;

- Both groups should try to identify common criteria or principles rather than those that are specific to the situation or case;

- Both groups should think in terms of an overall, generic framework for the recommended indicators, rather than simply a list of particular indicators;

- Participants were encouraged to flag research issues as they were encountered and to list follow-up research projects;

- The working groups were to build on the concepts, ideas, and examples arising from the computer conference, especially those dealing with benefits and indicators;

- Both groups were admonished to document their working assumptions, including the parameters and variables on which key decisions and conclusion were based;

- The case studies were to be used to "anchor" the analysis, conclusions, and recommendations in the real world;

- The case studies were to be used primarily as points of reference; the groups were asked not to assess their strengths and weaknesses; and

- The case studies were not to be considered the only points of reference — other cases could be raised in the deliberations.

From the third session on the first day of the workshop through the following day, the two groups worked independently. Each decided upon its own methods and timetable. IDRC staff navigated between the two groups to act as facilitators. Considerable interaction also took place among the participants between sessions and the working groups eventually held sessions in the evenings.

At the end of the second day, participants assembled in a plenary session to present a brief summary of the approaches and findings of the working groups. Later, the chairpersons, rapporteurs, and the consultant met to prepare a draft summary of the findings on posters, which were displayed on the walls of the main meeting room.

The third day began with a presentation by the Honourable Betty Bigombe, Mininster of State for Uganda, on the role, value, and limitations of information for those at the highest levels of policy- and decision-making. The reports of the working groups were pre- sented, and conclusions and suggestions for future activities were discussed. The rapporteurs of the working groups agreed to prepare individual reports of the deliberations of each group and an inte- grated report.

Proceedings of the working groups

The findings and recommendations of both working groups have been incorporated into a preliminary framework for impact assess- ment (Chapter 6) and suggestions for future activities (Chapter 7). Here we summarize the approach and process by which the groups arrived at their conclusions as background against which to inter- pret them.

Working group 1

Group 1 decided to make explicit working assumptions at a fairly general level; these could be referred to later if disagreement or confusion arose and adjusted if necessary. The members of the group listed two sets of assumptions about the nature and role of information that must form the basis for the development of assess- ment indicators for information projects. A third set of assumptions dealing with the concept of indicators (why are they needed and what are they used for) was also prepared (see Chapter 6).

An interesting discussion began as an attempt to identify the components of the "existing infrastructure capacities" on which an information project would be expected to be established, and from which it would draw support throughout its duration. Only much later did the group realize that this framework for identifying infrastructure capacity could become a framework for developing assessment indicators for inputs.

The group spent day 2 refining this indicators framework. Six categories were identified (later extended to eight). Much time was spent listing illustrative elements within each of the eight categories. The goal was to develop one or more indicators for each element (see Table 3). Time constraints prevented the preparation of a definitive list, but it was intended to be representative, containing illustrative entries that needed refinement. No attempt was made (again because of time limitations) to set priorities among the items in each category or rationalize their sequence, although from time to time the rapporteur was asked to move an item to a more logical position.

Attention turned to the output side after items under each of the eight categories in the indicators framework had been "fleshed out." An early attempt had been made to list expected outcomes; at one point "expected outcomes" was a ninth category in the framework when it was still hoped that a single, unified list of factors could serve both input and output sides in developing indicators. However, the group realized that expected outcomes (or "general benefit categories" as they were also called) should constitute a second list, and that a second step would be required to juxtapose the eight input indicator categories against the output categories. At least five major categories of benefits (outputs) were listed, with provision for additional ones.

An input–output matrix was designed to juxtapose the input resource categories with the benefit areas (see Table 4). After further discussion, it was agreed that two additional points had to be covered. First, the benefit areas should be further divided into two subcategories, quantifiable and nonquantifiable (or quantitative and qualitative). Second, the input indicators must be weighted according to some simple scale, say 1 to 5, based on how critical and relevant they are in assessing the success or failure of the project as a whole. The group then turned to devising and illustrating a three-step iterative procedure for using the proposed matrix in an impact assessment exercise (see Tables 4–6).

Participants also addressed the question of follow-up activities, including areas for further research. Four were identified: sustainability, benefit–cost study, information as a commodity, and cross-cultural impact assessment.

Working group 2

Group 2 began by developing a set of basic working assumptions about the assessment process. Members recognized that many different groups might be interested in the results of the assessment and identified five major ones whose special needs should be taken into account.

The group discussed and defined a process for developing assessment indicators. The first step was to address prerequisites for assessment. These were based in part on the results of the computer conference and on various assumptions about the assessment process that each group member raised in the discussion. The group produced a tentative list of those prerequisites.

Participants then outlined the steps to be taken in working collaboratively with representatives of the beneficiary groups with a view to determining the perceived benefits of information activities and products. It was concluded that a similar process may be required from the perspective of information needs and behaviour.

The group defined a model for assessment that was linked to the work of Griffiths and King (1993, fig. 18). The model consisted of four major components: the object(s) assessment perspectives, generic types of assessment measures, derived measures or indicators, and interactions and external factors. To test this framework, the group prepared examples of the types of assessment measures and indicators that could be applied to the CARICOM case study. It then attempted to match the various indicator types with the defined target audiences. This resulted in a matrix specifying the types of indicators that are more likely to be relevant for each of the major user groups identified (see Table 7).

The group ended its deliberations with a discussion of potential follow-up activities. It stressed the need for ensuring the consolidation and dissemination of impact assessment methods, as well as appropriate communication strategies for their results, through publications, manuals, and training. It concluded that a suitable mechanism for capturing, disseminating, and synthesizing assessment methods and their results is required.

Chapter 6

PRELIMINARY FRAMEWORK FOR IMPACT ASSESSMENT

———————■———————

The conclusions of the two working groups at the post-conference workshop and their discussion in plenary session form the basis for the synthesis presented in this chapter.

Basic assumptions

All efforts at developing indicators for the assessment of information activities and projects must be based on three sets of assumptions. They deal with the nature of information, its role, and the concept and functions of indicators.

Assumptions about the nature of information

- Information is a strategic resource that is critical to all levels, sectors, and endeavours of society, including development.

- Information must be communicated interactively from sender to receiver; information cannot be regarded as passive transfer of data. Ideally, there should be regular feedback from receiver to sender.

- Like all resources, information has both unique and common attributes. Added value increases with use; unlike most other resources, the more information is used, the more valuable it becomes.

- Information, like most other resources, has a life cycle and value is added at each stage. The notion of an information "food chain" is a useful metaphor. Information is less time-sensitive than most other resources.

- The full value of information includes both its present value and its potential value, which is not always readily discernible.

- To exploit its maximum value, information must be managed, beginning at the level of the individual, then proceeding to the group level, the organization and institution, the country, the region, and finally the international and global level.

- Information is an instrument of power.

- Information has both benefits and costs, and they are often masked. Information is never a free good; someone, sometime, somewhere must pay for it.

- An effective and efficient information environment requires investment in human, physical, financial, and technological infrastructure. Information resources do not stand alone, out of context with other resources.

Assumptions about the role of information

- Information is produced or collected to satisfy societal needs at all levels, recognizing that "society" is a heterogeneous concept and that information can be misused.

- Societal needs are satisfied through various kinds of activities, each of which requires information as an input. These include, for example, education, policy formulation, research and development, personal needs, business decision-making, mass communications, public goods, and private goods.

- Societal needs are also satisfied at different levels, from individuals through to global communities.

Assumptions about indicators and their functions

■ Indicators are needed to identify, measure, and evaluate existing infrastructure capacities in the relevant sectors to absorb new resource inputs and to achieve expected results (outputs).

■ Indicators are also needed to determine the degree to which a project or activity succeeds or fails in meeting stated general needs and objectives, in using resources efficiently, and in achieving expected results.

Furthermore, assessment of the impact of information cannot be a self-contained, one-time exercise. On the contrary, it should be based upon the following principles:

■ The assessment process must be beneficiary or user driven;

■ The target audiences (those who will use the results of the assessment) should be clearly identified from the outset;

■ Not all indicators will apply in any given situation;

■ Assessment is an ongoing process; and

■ Assessment should be built into project formulation, not added as an afterthought.

Many groups might be interested in the results of an impact assessment. However, five main categories of potential audiences can be identified: decision-makers, information managers, information and information-system users, the community at large, and donors or funding agencies.

Steps in the assessment process

Before undertaking an impact assessment, a number of prerequisites should be met. Based in part on the results of the computer conference and on various assumptions about the assessment process that were expressed at the post-conference workshop, the following prerequisites were established. The list is not necessarily exhaustive.

■ Define the user community.

- Define the development issue(s) and program(s) to which the information activity(ies) or project(s) in question are contributing.

- Identify the main patterns of operation of the global information life cycle and the factors that influence its effectiveness for the defined user community and issue.

- Describe target audiences (those who will use the indicators) for the results of the assessment.

- Describe the information use environments (IUEs) of the user community(ies) and the target audiences (see Chapter 4 for a detailed description of the IUE concept).

- Set up standard guidelines for collecting, analyzing, interpreting, and presenting anecdotes and other data.

- Assemble baseline data.

After the prerequisites have been met, it is necessary to work collaboratively with representatives of the beneficiary groups (both decision-makers and end-users) to determine the perceived or expected benefits of information activities and products.

Identification of the factors to be included in the framework, from the point of view of the provision of information, should follow these steps:

- Determine which primary objectives are being served (economic, social, political).

- Develop a nested hierarchy of objectives or outcomes; define outputs, establish input requirements, and specify other factors that influence the outcomes.

- At each level of the hierarchy, identify critical factors that are either informational in nature or information-dependent.

- Define the indicators in the framework that would show that the information input is secured and improved.

In some instances, for example, when the provision of information seems to be grossly inadequate or relies heavily on informal channels, a similar process may have to be followed from the perspective of information needs and behaviour. Its results may be either combined with those from the former perspective or substituted for them.

Overall structure of a framework for impact assessment

Based on the work of Griffiths and King (1993) and complemented by the results of the computer conference and the discussions at the post-conference workshop, the overall structure of a model for the assessment of the impact of information can be outlined (Figures 1–3). It contains four major components: the object of evaluation and evaluation perspectives; generic measures; derived measures or indicators; and interactions and external factors.

The object of the assessment can be any or a combination of several levels of information projects or activities, for example, an entire program, a specific project, or a specific service. Similarly, there are various assessment perspectives, such as the information service provider, the information service user, the beneficiary, and the donor or funding agency.

Generic assessment measures include inputs, outputs, usage, outcomes, and domain measures (Figure 1). Input measures relate to the amount, cost, and attributes of resources used to perform an activity, provide a service, produce a product, or operate a program. Output measures are concerned with the results of the application of the input resources; they can be measured in terms of the amount of output produced and by attributes of that output. Usage measures relate to the amount of use and nonuse, and factors affecting them. Outcome measures address the consequences of use of the information or information service. Finally, domain measures relate the characteristics of the environment within which the information projects or activities are implemented to their achievements.

The measures alone convey little information and, therefore, a more detailed assessment can be achieved through the development

```
┌─────────────────────────────────────────────────┐
│                Object of Evaluation               │
│  ■ Program ■ Project ■ Service ■ Activity ■ Resource ■ │
└─────────────────────────────────────────────────┘
```

**Evaluation
perspectives**   **Measures**

Inputs (resources)
- Amount of resources
- Cost of resources
- Attributes

**Information
service
provider**

Outputs (products and services)
- Amount of output
- Attributes of output
  - Quality
  - Timeliness
  - Availability
  - Accessibility

**User
(actual and
potential)**

Usage
- Amount of use and nonuse
- Factors affecting use and
  nonuse
  - Purpose of use
  - Importance
  - Satisfaction with attributes
    of output
  - Awareness
  - Ease and cost of use

Beneficiary

Outcomes (consequences
of use and nonuse)
- Time saved
- Improved productivity
- Improved quality of work
- Improved timeliness of work
- Value derived

**Donor
agency**

Domain (environmental characteristics)
- Target population
- User and nonuser population
- User and nonuser information needs
- Number and attributes of sites

Society

Figure 1. Conceptual framework for impact assessment:
evaluation perspectives and measures.

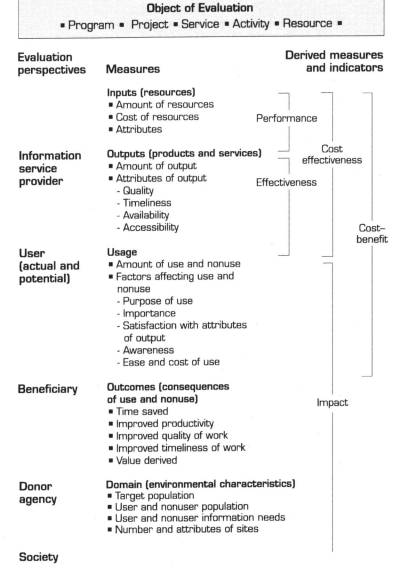

Figure 2. Conceptual framework for impact assessment: derived measures and indicators.

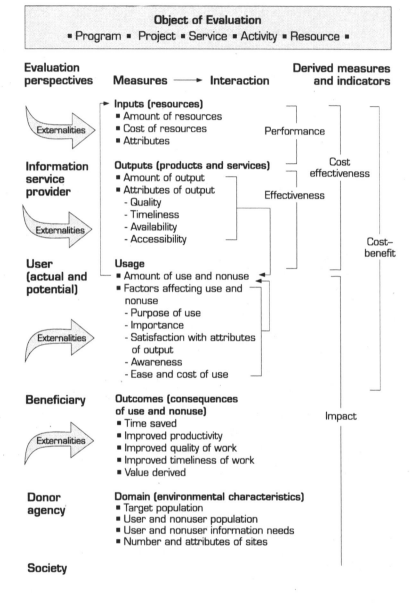

Figure 3. Conceptual framework for impact assessment:
interaction and externalities.

of derived measures or indicators for assessment. Figure 2 shows five types of assessment indicators:

- Performance indicators relating inputs to outputs;
- Effectiveness indicators relating outputs to usage;
- Cost-effectiveness indicators relating inputs to usage;
- Cost–benefit indicators relating inputs to outcomes; and
- Impact indicators relating usage to outcomes and domain characteristics.

There is an interactive effect or feedback mechanism built into the model since changes in one component are likely to reflect in others. Changes in input or output attributes should affect usage. Increased usage requires modified inputs to produce modified outputs. Also, changes in conditions that affect usage will also affect input and output requirements.

External factors also affect the measurements at all levels (Figure 3). These are often beyond the control of the assessor, but play an increasingly important part in outcomes as the measurement moves from the top part of the model to the bottom. One area for future research identified by the group is how to determine causality at these higher levels of assessment.

Input and output categories to be considered in the framework

Information activities and projects are based on an existing information infrastructure and draw upon its components for support throughout their duration. The following input categories should be considered: human factors; information and communications technologies; systems and processes; financial aspects; plant capacity; external links and distribution; policy and environment; and users. For each category, a list of the main characteristics that should be reflected in appropriate indicators is proposed below (Table 3). It is by no means definitive. Rather, it is intended to be representative;

Table 3. Characteristics in each of the defined input categories that require assessment indicators.

Category	Characteristic requiring appropriate indicator
Human factors	Technical knowledge, competence, and skill
	Management and leadership knowledge, competence, and skill
	Access to education and training facilities
	Behavioural parameters (sociopsychological variables, including attitude)
	Available manpower (including productivity)
	Demographic considerations
	Socioeconomic parameters (including rewards, status, income, etc.)
	Personnel security (e.g., clearances for sensitive positions)
	Cross-cultural factors (including race, religion, ethnicity, age, and sex, values and beliefs)
Information and communications technologies	Computers and automatic data processing (including micro-electronics and associated equipment, all collection, storage, retrieval, and dissemination media and modes such as CD-ROM and optical discs)
	Telecommunications network linkages (local and wide band)
	Software (standard and customized)
	Man–machine interfaces (e.g., user friendliness)
	Ergonomic factors
	Media facilities
	Indigenous technologies
	Technical support
	Local manufacturing, distribution, and supply
Systems and processes	Existing information flows (baseline requirements, including information content)
	System requirements
	Inputs (including data collection)
	Throughputs
	Outputs (including products and services)
	Feedback loops (both positive and negative)
	Organizational dynamics
	Procedures
	Safeguards
Financial aspects	Direct and indirect costs
	Quantifiable and nonquantifiable costs
	Recurring and nonrecurring costs
	Current operating expenses
	Capital investments
	Hidden costs
	Recoverable and sunk (nonrecoverable) costs
	Pricing
	Worth (subjective value)
	Savings (benefits)

(continued)

Table 3 concluded.

Category	Characteristic requiring appropriate indicator
Plant capacity	Space planning and design
	Engineering, ventilation, and electricals
	Communications
	Lighting
	Maintenance
	Plumbing
	Furniture and equipment
	Supplies and materials
	Location (accessibility)
	Security
	Obsolescence and depreciation
External linkages and distribution	Information, communications, and telecommunications networks at the global, regional, national, and local levels
	Institutional networks at the global, regional, national, and local levels
	Individual networks at the global, regional, national, and local levels
	Public (constituencies and clienteles)
	Beneficiaries
Policy and environmental factors	Political commitment
	National support capacity
	Appropriate national information policies
	Commitment of top management
	Organizational culture
	Societal culture
	Political culture and climate
	Economic culture and climate (including funding opportunities)
	Physical environment
	Ethical considerations
Users	Needs assessment
	User(s) profile(s) and entry points
	Motivation, attitudes, behaviour
	Awareness and literacy level
	Education and training
	Access and exposure
	Use and adoption
	Feedback channels
	Willingness and ability to pay
	User constraints
	User satisfaction

the illustrative entries need refinement. No attempt was made to set priorities or establish the sequence of the items in each category.

On the outcome side, an initial list of five general categories of benefits was devised, recognizing that additional ones might be required: political, economic, social, cultural, and technological benefits. These areas should be further divided into two sub-categories, quantifiable and nonquantifiable, or quantitative and qualitative.

Linking input and output categories

A matrix of the input categories and output benefit areas was prepared to provide a canvas for identifying the interactions between them. The input indicators must be weighted on a simple scale according to how critical and relevant they are to the success of the activity or project as a whole. This is a measure of the strength of the relation between the indicators in the input areas and one of the five major output benefit areas. A suitable scale might be as follows: 1, weak correlation; 2, below average; 3, average; 4, above average; and 5, strong correlation.

Tables 4, 5, and 6 illustrate the steps by which the matrix could be filled in through an iterative process. The data and check marks in the cells are illustrative only; they are by no means prescriptive.

- Step 1: Put an X or check mark in the cells that are functionally appropriate and relevant. Do not worry about weighting the input–output relation at this stage. Simply note that such a relation exists (Table 4).

- Step 2: Darken the Xs or check marks to indicate a strong correlation, as an intermediate step before moving toward a final weighted score using the 1–5 scale (Table 5).

- Step 3: Estimate the strength of the input–output relation using the scale (Table 6).

Communicating the results

Not all indicators will be relevant to all audiences. However, information managers should be interested in all categories of indicators and all audiences might be interested in the impact indicators. Table 7 shows an example of how the match could be depicted.

Table 4. Step 1: the input–output matrix.
Relationship (X) between input and output categories.

Input factors	Output benefits[a]									
	Political		Economic		Social		Cultural		Technological	
	Qt	Ql	Qt	Ql	Qt	Ql	Qt	Ql	Qt	Ql
Human	X		X		X		X			
Information and communication technologies									X	
Systems and processes			X	X	X	X	X	X		
Financial			X	X						
Plant capacity			X	X					X	X
External links and distribution		X	X	X	X	X	X	X		
Policy and environment	X	X	X	X	X	X	X	X	X	X
Users			X	X	X	X	X	X	X	X

[a] Qt, quantitative; Ql, qualitative.

Table 5. Step 2: the input–output matrix.
Strength of relationship (**X**, strong) between input and output categories.

Input factors	Output benefits[a]									
	Political		Economic		Social		Cultural		Technological	
	Qt	Ql	Qt	Ql	Qt	Ql	Qt	Ql	Qt	Ql
Human	X		X		**X**		**X**			
Information and communication technologies									**X**	
Systems and processes			X	X	X	X	X	X		
Financial			**X**	X						
Plant capacity			X	**X**					**X**	**X**
External links and distribution		**X**	X	X	X	X	X	X		
Policy and environment	**X**	**X**	X	X	X	X	X	X	X	X
Users			**X**	X	**X**	X	**X**	X	X	X

[a] Qt, quantitative; Ql, qualitative.

Table 6. Step 3: the input–output matrix. Estimated correlation between input and output categories on a scale of 1 to 5.

Input factors	Political Qt	Political Ql	Economic Qt	Economic Ql	Social Qt	Social Ql	Cultural Qt	Cultural Ql	Technological Qt	Technological Ql
Human	3		3			5		4		
Information and communication technologies									4	
Systems and processes			2	3	3	3	2	3		
Financial			5	2						
Plant capacity			3	4					5	4
External links and distribution		4	1	2	2	1	2	3		
Policy and environment	4	5	3	3	3	2	2	3	3	3
Users			4	2	5	2	5	3	3	3

[a] Qt, quantitative; Ql, qualitative.

Table 7. Matching the categories of assessment indicators with the main target audiences.

Audience	Operational, performance	Effectiveness	Impact	Cost
Decision-makers	?	?	✓	✓
Information managers	✓	✓	✓	✓
Users	?	✓	✓	✓
Community as a whole	?	?	✓	✓
Donors	?	?	✓	?

The target audiences must be identified early in the assessment process. Their unique perception of the critical issues and the benefits resulting from information should be determined, so that relevant indicators can be devised and included in the exercise. When the analysis is complete, the results should be checked against these requirements and packaged appropriately for each group to enhance their effective communication.

The framework devised by the working groups was tested during the post-conference workshop using an IDRC-funded project called Information for Decision-Making in the Caribbean Community (Appendix 5). Examples of the types of assessment measures and indicators that could be applied were identified. In addition, the application of the overall method to the CARICOM project was examined in greater detail at a subsequent meeting in Jamaica.

Chapter 7

SUGGESTIONS FOR FUTURE ACTIVITIES

———————■———————

Follow-up activities

Dissemination

In addition to this publication, the results of our project will be disseminated by the participants through individual publications and presentations at conferences. These communications will increase awareness of the subject and interest in continuing its study.

Impact assessment methods may be disseminated among the communities concerned, for example, through workshops, consultations, and informal interaction with those already active in the area.

Initial field testing

On the basis of the material reported here, impact assessments will be designed and implemented in a number of IDRC-funded projects as the next phase of this investigation. These field tests will take place within different geographical, sectoral, and user environments. For example, one of the first to be supported will be the CARICOM project described in Appendix 5, which will examine the impact of several regional information systems as perceived by different user communities in the Caribbean. Another field test will examine in more detail the impact of a regional single-sector information system on the decisions of senior policymakers; this is the education information network operated across Latin America by the Centro de Investigación y Desarrollo de la Educación in Santiago, Chile. Other case studies under discussion include an information system designed to serve a national legislature, a specialized information centre serving an international research program, and a technology information service intended to benefit rural communities. These initial field tests supported by IDRC will be taking place over the next 2 or 3 years. Other agencies and organizations may wish to consider similar exercises in conjunction with their own projects and according to their own concerns. Related studies might also be undertaken as research projects or assignments to graduate students.

Training

Appropriate formats and methods for presenting the results of impact assessments to the various target audiences should be explored, tested, and documented; feedback should be monitored and used to improve them. This is a critical step in the overall process; the full benefits of an increased understanding of the impact of information on development will only be realized if the findings can be conveyed effectively to the appropriate target audiences for further action and reinforcement.

Developing a training package might be worthwhile in terms of streamlining transfer of the concepts and methods. Although not a prerequisite for field-testing, consolidation of the material available as a result of the project in the form of practical handbooks would be helpful. For example, guidelines for defining, collecting, analyzing, interpreting, and presenting anecdotes and other data are required, especially by organizations in developing countries, for eventual impact assessments as well as for their own strategic management; these would facilitate the design of field tests and help ensure the minimum level of consistency required for comparison of their results. An expanded version of the criteria and framework for conducting impact assessments contained in this report, with practical examples and more detailed guidance, would probably be welcomed by organizations in developing countries that would like to undertake such exercises.

Cost–benefit analysis

The proposed framework for impact assessment relies to a significant extent upon the concepts and methods used in cost– benefit analysis. A handbook on the application of this methodology to information projects in developing countries, based upon one or several case studies, would permit a more standardized approach. Its description in practical terms would facilitate field-testing. Cost–benefit analysis might also be used as a standard component of project formulation and evaluation.

IDRC has initiated some work on producing a practical handbook on how to apply cost–benefit analysis to information projects. The guide is intended primarily for use in developing countries; it will incorporate the concepts presented in this report and be tested in a real project setting.

Further studies

Systematic testing and analysis

The next step in the effort initiated by this project should be concentrated on gathering empirical data, validating the concepts and methods, and gaining further insight into the issues. This can best be achieved by testing the proposed methods for measuring the impact of information on development in selected information use environments (IUEs) and in relation to specific problems identified by the communities in them. The choice of the environments will depend on existing projects or institutional support. The choice of methods, from among those mentioned in this report and others, will depend on the specific environment and problem.

Even if the project's findings are consolidated as suggested above, continuation of this long-term effort will probably go through a stage of somewhat random application from the point of view of sophistication of methods and choice of subjects. To avoid unnecessary duplication and fragmentation of efforts, a tentative list of IUEs and priority issues should be drawn up as soon as possible. From the first round of field tests, basic guidelines for the description of IUEs and various approaches to the assessment of the impact of information can be developed. If preliminary versions have already been produced, they can be revised and updated. This may be regarded as a priority objective at this stage.

While field tests are being carried out, even if they are based on tentative assumptions and designs, it would be advisable to broadcast their framework widely among agencies supporting information projects, the information community, and academic institutions to maximize the possibility of related investigations, even of a limited scope. At this stage, agencies embarking on information-related projects might be in a position to include at the formulation phase a thorough audit of the existing situation regarding information, a description of the related IUEs, and cost–benefit analysis of their projects, if applicable. A reasonable proportion of the projects should include such components. Although fieldwork on assessing the impact of information and related studies will presumably increase, we hope that those involved in such endeavours will take advantage of the expertise of the participants in the original project.

Monitoring and evaluation

Current and future efforts, as well as past ones, should be monitored, at least through reviews of the literature, but more usefully through site visits and seminars. Such monitoring will facilitate the process of evaluating and consolidating relevant experience and streamline comparisons among the various studies. In the design of research protocols, for example, this would ensure compatibility among the various assessments, comparison and discussion of results, and selection of the constituencies to be investigated. If concerned teams had access to an electronic network, their interaction as well as the effectiveness of their work would be greatly enhanced.

An effort to map all significant IUEs would be worthwhile at this stage. This process will be long term and open ended and its effectiveness will depend on appropriate communications among those involved. Even if monitoring and evaluation of the various individual impact-assessment projects takes place, after about 5 years their findings should be discussed at a workshop and consolidated in a report. This would allow researchers to compare results and methods, refine them, and revise the handbooks. If a sufficient number of assessments have been successfully carried out during what may be considered the field-testing phase, the methods could be revised and subsequent assessments could encompass validation of the results of the earlier studies. Upon completion of this new round of fieldwork, a second summary of the results would be appropriate, including further revision of the handbooks.

Although there seems to be a consensus about the need to begin with micro-level studies before considering such macro-level issues as benefit at the national level for a particular sector or in relation to major development priorities, a prospective study might be worthwhile to provide an outline of possible macro-level benefits. This would result in a series of hypotheses that could aid in the design of micro-level studies and later be checked against their results. To the extent that a number of decisions regarding investment in information are taken at the macro-level (for example, programs to help countries move toward an information-based economy), the outline might, if used with caution, prove useful for practical and methodological purposes.

The need for a cooperative program

Given the size and complexity of the problem of measuring the impact of information and the required bottom-up approach, if only a few organizations are involved in such studies there is likely to be a long delay in obtaining significant results. By that time, the information gap between the North and the South may have widened so much that developing countries may not be able to correct the imbalance. Therefore, this subject should become the theme of an international program, involving a large number of institutions, North and South. Cooperation would allow the various groups to harmonize their approaches, combine their respective efforts, achieve a more thorough coverage of the various problems, constituencies, and geographic areas, and exchange results and observations. Aside from communication costs and adequate monitoring of the related projects at all stages, this cooperation does not imply significant expense. The program could operate as a decentralized network.

Industrialized countries currently invest considerable amounts of money in information research of which little, if any, is applied to the investigation of information problems in developing countries. Are incremental steps toward the sophistication of information storage and retrieval so important that they cannot be delayed in favour of studies that could bring about a better global balance in the provision and use of information? A better understanding of the role of information in developing countries could be of direct value to the industrialized countries. Programs supporting research in information sciences should, therefore, earmark resources specifically for the study of information activities in developing countries, including impact assessment.

An increasing number of students from developing countries are enrolling in doctoral programs in industrialized countries. This creates an enormous research potential that is currently misused in work that too often has no direct relevance for developing countries, but reinforces the advantage of industrialized countries. If an international program of research is properly publicized, some of this potential may be directed toward it. To that end, the program should establish appropriate links with the concerned doctoral programs and research funding agencies.

Baseline studies and data gathering could also be assigned to students in developing countries, under appropriate supervision. Such work would contribute more to their intellectual background and to advances in the field than the usual inconsistent descriptions of particular information services.

As previously mentioned, the formulation of information projects could also offer a unique opportunity for carrying out some of the required studies. The participation of agencies that support such projects would, thus, be highly desirable.

Additional research

Based on the results of the project, a number of issues have been raised that require theoretical and applied research. The findings should be reviewed with a view to drawing up a list of possible research topics. Some points have already been noted by various participants. For example, some believe that there is a need to clarify the basic concept of "sustainability" of information systems and services. Its frequent use seems to imply that some information projects or activities may not be sustainable. It is important to examine the conditions for achieving sustainability and the eventual limits of the concept. This is a field of research that is of increasing interest to IDRC (Agha 1992; Agha and Akhtar 1992).

Both the computer conference and post-conference workshop focused on information as a resource rather than a commodity. However, developing countries, as well as others, can profit, literally, from income generated by information sales as an end or intermediate product or service, in both internal and international markets. This issue, which was only alluded to during the computer conference, should be explored thoroughly.

The impact of information, because of its pervasiveness and complexity, may be subjected to other forms of analysis such as those used in studies of environmental impact in a cross- or multicultural context. Comparative studies of such methods could evolve into a guide for project planning and evaluation.

Observations regarding the impact of information must be made at an appropriate level of aggregation, so that the number of significant factors and the external factors that may affect them are not grossly simplified. One must observe the interaction of factors and the co-occurrence of effects or events within a relatively complex set. A key research issue is whether it is possible, if not to establish causality, then at least to reduce the uncertainty about the meaning and direction of these interactions.

A number of theoretical questions underlie the concepts, criteria, framework, and methods for impact assessment presented in this report. To a large extent, assessing the impact of information implies that the value of information is defined, which will lead to some definition of information itself. How to move from the model of discrete messages, where information theory has been deadlocked, to an acceptable representation of a plurality of messages and uses, which is the common experience of individuals and groups, is probably the more significant and challenging of these problems.

Outcome of the project

Although it considered all possible facets of the relation between information and development, the computer conference was intended to be a brainstorming session and preliminary investigation. Its outcome was encouraging. The project and its scope may have generated unrealistic expectations within the community, including among the participants themselves. However, there was no intention, nor would it have been possible, to go beyond the production of a comprehensive and articulated framework, description of critical issues, and identification of a number of hypotheses, to produce indicators that could provide evidence of the positive role of information in development.

The subject is indeed complex, difficult to tackle, and unusual. It requires breaking away from established concepts, concerns, and methods. Of particular significance is the need to question the assumption that information comes from the formal information sector, which has so far dominated the analysis of the "information society" in industrialized countries. Change in this field is no longer about the mode of production of material goods; it is about ways of thinking and, therefore, reminding us of Descartes, about the essence of individuals and societies. The computer conference achieved what it set out to do. The avenues it has opened for future investigations are clear, rich, and promising. We can no longer be satisfied with the endless repetition of the axiom that information is an essential resource for development. Solid evidence must be gathered and shaped. The conference took a first step and offered suggestions for further research in this area.

During the conference, the time devoted to various points was not uniform; some issues were omitted, some ideas need further elaboration, and too many directions were indicated. Although many points raised during the conference are probably not new for the specialist, the comprehensive discussion of the trade-offs between information and development and avenues for their investigation may offer a new outlook. We hope that many specialists will find a wide range of ideas worth exploring in this report, as well as inspiration and challenge for embarking on the endeavour. If so, the conference will have achieved its other target — to set the pace for studying the role of information in development.

Although it was linked with the computer conference, the post-conference workshop demonstrated that a suitable starting point had been created. Most of the participants who had not been closely associated with the computer conference were clearly comfortable with its findings. They quickly took up the task that had been assigned to them and went through a process that was expected to be difficult with amazing ease.

Each of the working groups took a particular approach and focused on specific aspects of the task. However, their conclusions were so coherent and complementary that the resulting synthesis developed naturally. The framework for assessment, and the stepwise approach to using it, produced at the post-conference workshop, are articulate, appropriate, and effective. The framework and process must now be refined and applied in particular contexts. Because they were based on actual cases, this stage should present no serious problem. Actual field tests are all that is now required for their validation and improvement.

People may argue that this report does not contain a prescriptive list of indicators. Others may complain that it does not provide answers to all the questions they are facing, some of which they cannot even articulate. In both cases, they may have misunderstood the nature of the problem. It is fortunate that the project did not provide such answers. It is up to the people who are meant to benefit from information to specify the criteria to be used to verify whether those benefits have been realized.

This project serves as a starting point. It has developed a method for carrying out assessments and criteria for selecting, organizing, and presenting indicators. It is now possible to undertake further studies, both empirical ones in the field and theoretical ones, to reach progressively a better understanding of the role of information in development and to refine the methods of investigation.

LIST OF PARTICIPANTS

———————■———————

This Appendix lists the participants and contributors to the computer conference and post-conference workshop, as follows: *, participant (regular or occasional) in the computer conference; ‡, member of the consultative panel; §, participant in the post-conference workshop.

Wilson O. **Aiyepeku**[‡§]
Director
Africa Regional Centre for Information Sciences
University of Ibadan
Ibadan, Nigeria

Toni Carbo **Bearman**[*]
Dean and Professor
School of Library and Information Science
University of Pittsburgh
Pittsburgh, PA, USA

Betty **Bigombe**[§]
Minister of State
Prime Minister's Office
Kampala, Uganda

John B. **Black**[*]
Chief Librarian
McLaughlin Library
University of Guelph
Guelph, ON, Canada

Cecil **Blake**[§]
International Development Research Centre
Regional Office for Eastern and Southern Africa
Nairobi, Kenya

Antonio A. **Briquet de Lemos**[*]
Consultant
Retired Head of Publications Department
University of Brasilia
Brasília, Brasil

Cornelius (Neil) **Burk**, Jr[*]
Information Management and Technology Consultants
Ottawa, ON, Canada

Patricio **Cariola**, S.J.[‡]
Director
Centro de Investigación y Desarrollo de la Educación
Santiago, Chile

Carol **Collins**[§]
Information Resources Manager
CARICOM Secretariat
Georgetown, Guyana

Blaise **Cronin**[*]
Dean
School of Library and Information Science
Indiana University
Bloomington, IN, USA

Julio **Cubillo**[*][§]
Regional Adviser
Centro Latino Americano de Documentación Económica y Social
UN/CEPAL
Santiago, Chile

Marta **Dosa**[‡]
Professor Emeritus
School of Information Studies
Syracuse University
Syracuse, NY, USA

Nathalie **Dussoulier**[§]
Vice President
INIST Group
Vandoeuvre-lès-Nancy, France

Stephney **Ferguson***[§]
Head
Department of Library Studies
University of the West Indies
Kingston, Jamaica

José-Marie **Griffiths***[§]
Director
Centre for Information Studies
University of Tennessee
Knoxville, TN, USA

Nagy **Hanna**[‡]
Senior Economist
World Bank
Washington, DC, USA

L.J. **Haravu**[§]
Manager
Library and Documentation Services
International Crops Research Institute for the Semi-Arid Tropics
Andhra Pradesh, India

Forest Woody **Horton**, Jr*[§]
Information Management Press Inc.
Washington, DC, USA

F. Wilfred **Lancaster**[‡]
Professor Emeritus
Graduate School of Library and Information Science
University of Illinois at Urbana Champaign
Urbana, IL, USA

Robin **Mansell**[‡]
Head
Centre for Information and Communication Technologies
Science Policy Research Unit
University of Sussex
Brighton, UK

Paul **McConnell**[§]
Director
Program Coordination and Development
Information Sciences and Systems Division
International Development Research Centre
Ottawa, ON, Canada

Kingo **Mchombu**[‡§]
Lecturer
Department of Library Studies
University of Botswana
Gaborone, Botswana

Michel J. **Menou**[*§]
Consultant in Information Management Systems
Gentilly, France

Enzo **Molino**[*]
Centro de Estudios Eléctricas
Mexico DF, Mexico

Youssef **Nusseir**[*]
Director
Information and Computer Software Centre
Royal Scientific Society
Amman, Jordan

Anna Maria **Pratt**[‡]
Comision Nacional de Investigacion Cientifica y Tecnologica
Santiago, Chile

Jean **Salmona**[*]
Director General
Data for Development
Marseille, France

Rojan **Samarajiva**[*]
Department of Communication
Ohio State University
Colombus, OH, USA

Tefko **Saracevic**[‡]
Distinguished Professor
School of Communication, Information and Library Studies
Rutgers University
New Brunswick, NJ, USA

Martha B. **Stone**[*][§]
Director General
Information Sciences and Systems Division
International Development Research Centre
Ottawa, ON, Canada

Karl **Stroetmann**[‡]
Consultant
Alfter, Germany

Robert S. **Taylor**[‡]
Professor Emeritus
School of Information Studies
Syracuse University
Syracuse, NY, USA

Louis **Vagianos**[§]
IDRC Consultant
Blandford Information Specialists
Toronto, ON, Canada

Arthur **Vespry**[‡]
Director,
Library and Regional Documentation Centre
Asian Institute of Technology
Bangkok, Thailand

Robert A. **Vitro**[*]
Director
Global Business Development
Information Industry Association
Washington, DC, USA

Nancy M. **Wildgoose**[‡]
Director General Policy Coordination
Policy and Communications
National Defence Headquarters
Ottawa, ON, Canada

    The editor also wishes to acknowledge the additional contributions he received from the following individuals: Raymond Aubrac (Information Consultant, Paris, France), Judith Carrie (IWG Canada Inc., Calgary, AB, Canada), Elizabeth Cockburn (University of Guelph, Guelph, ON, Canada), Harry Cummings (University of Guelph, Guelph, ON, Canada), Madjid Dahmane (Research Centre on Scientific and Technical Information, Algiers, Algeria), Allen G. Dyer (University of Guelph, Guelph, ON, Canada), Oswald Ganley (Harvard University, Cambridge, MA, USA), John N. Gathegi (Florida State University, Tallahassee, FL, USA), Peter Havard-Williams (University of Botswana, Gaborone, Botswana), Seppo Heikinnen (Unesco, Santiago, Chile), Marianne Logelin (Université de Bordeaux III, Bordeaux, France), Ian Miles (University of Manchester, Manchester, UK), Richard Neill (University of Botswana, Gaborone, Botswana), Stephen Parker (*Information Development*, Colombo, Sri Lanka), Ernesto Schiefelbein (Unesco, Santiago, Chile), Vladimir Slamecka (Georgia Institute of Technology, Atlanta, GA, USA), and Sherill Weaver-Wozniak (Indiana University, Bloomington, IN, USA).

APPLYING CBA TO AN
INFORMATION PROJECT

—————■—————

Step 1. Define the objectives

Overall objective: To create a national database, information system, and clearinghouse for acquired immune deficiency syndrome (AIDS) to be used as a national information asset, available to and accessible by

- Accredited national, regional, and international public health institutions and organizations,

- Authorized practising public and other health professionals,

- Qualified academic public and other health research facilities,

- Public health and health-related government departments, and

- Other users and beneficiaries on an "as entitled and as needed" basis.

Long-term goal (at the level of education and enlightenment; substantial achievement to take 10 years or longer): To decrease the incidence of endemic AIDS in the population from $X\%$ to $Y\%$ by the end of the out-year period (10 or more years) by creating conditions that allow high-risk populations to become fully aware of the political, economic, social, and human consequences of dysfunctional attitudes and behaviour, including life-style, values, and beliefs.

Mid-term goal (at the level of helping information; substantial achievement in 5 to 10 years): To increase the awareness of high-risk populations of dysfunctional attitudes and behaviour from *A*% to *B*% per year over the projected 5 to 10 years.

Short-term goal (at the coping level; substantial achievement by the end of the 4th year): To sensitize the target public health user and beneficiary groups to the existence of the new information resources (the database, the information system, and the clearinghouse), availability and accessibility conditions or preconditions, their responsibilities for both data input and data use, and other awareness factors, so that 95% of all target groups are fully aware of the resource and are using the information assets (knowledge, expertise, and facilities) in an effective, fully-functioning manner.

Step 2. Formulate assumptions

Increase in workload: The number of new items added to the database will be — to — in the first year after it becomes fully operational (Stage I, database creation and bringing it on line), — to — for the next *X* years (Stage II, rapid growth), — to — for the next *Y* years (Stage III, levelling off), and is extrapolated to grow from — to — per year following year 10 (or longer) when the database is mature.

Volume of user demand: Demands from users for access and retrieval of items from the database will increase from — to — in the first year, etc. (following the pattern outlined under *Increase in workload* above).

Life cycle of the resource: The database, information system, and clearinghouse are expected to remain fully functional without requiring major modification until year 10 (or longer). Thereafter a new CBA will be required to take advantage of new technology, new approaches, and changes in user demand patterns.

Period covered by the analysis: A 10-year life cycle was selected on the grounds that the resource's capabilities and technological infrastructure would remain relatively stable during that time.

Inflation rate adjustment: An inflation rate of $X\%$ per year was used to project quantified benefits and costs over the life cycle of the system.

Salary cost projection: Base rates used to calculate salaries were considered to rise by $A\%$ during the first 3 years of the project; $B\%$ for the next 3 years; and $C\%$ for the remaining 4 years.

Step 3. Identify alternatives

Status quo: Do not create a new information resource. This alternative may be considered the baseline.

Modify existing system: Maintain the current approach, but make modest changes to upgrade its efficiency and effectiveness.

Create new database, information system, and clearinghouse: Create a brand new capability and gradually phase out the old approach and replace it with the new one. Running the old and new systems in parallel for 1 or 2 years may be required.

Step 4. Estimate benefits or values and costs or burdens

- Categorize benefits as quantifiable or nonquantifiable.

- Distinguish between recurring and nonrecurring benefits.

- Project benefits year-by-year for the life cycle of the project. Some benefits may be the same each year, but others may change as the project matures.

- Distinguish between efficiency benefits and effectiveness benefits. The former help do the same jobs better at the same or reduced cost by using a different technique, approach, or method; the latter help do new and different jobs. These are benefits to the producer or funder, but not necessarily to the user.

Table A1. Short-, mid-, and long-term assessment indicators.

Short-term indicators[a]

- Increased awareness (information literacy) by users and beneficiaries of the existence of, applications for, and methods for using the new information resource (33% awareness level achieved for target user populations by the end of 1st year)

- Operation of a single, central authoritative resource to replace a multiplicity of fragmented, dispersed, and ineffective resources

- Increased availability of the information to more users and clienteles

- Broader, faster and more effective access to the information resource

- Improved retrieval and delivery of documents

- Improved search capability

- Improved retrievability of data, documents, and literature

- Greater usefulness of the output from the information resource because of formatting and packaging features

- Decreased incidence of AIDS from X% to Y% (modest decrease)

Mid-term indicators[b]

- Faster and more effective application of knowledge to AIDS research

- Faster and more effective application of knowledge in AIDS public awareness programs

- Faster and more effective application of knowledge in AIDS education and training programs, both formal and informal

- Reduced time spent in searching for information from X to Y hours per day

- Reduced period between retrieval and application of information from X to Y hours per day

- Greater sharing of information among public health institutions and professionals

- Greater reuse of information assets

- Fewer instances of lost or missing information

- Awareness level of 66% achieved regarding existence of, applications for, and methods for using the new information resource in target user population

- More effective public policy decision-making

(continued)

Table A1 concluded.

Long-term indicators[c]

- Reduced incidence of AIDS from A % to B % in the primary target population as a whole

- Reduced incidence of AIDS from C % to D % in the target population at high risk

- Reduced incidence of AIDS from E % to F % in the secondary high-risk target population

- Awareness level of 95% achieved on existence of, applications for, and methods for using the new information resource in target user population

- Very effective public policy decision-making

---

[a] All but the last are related to the start-up process and how to use the new information resource, rather than the more substantive goals and objectives of the project.

[b] More equal balance between the mechanics of use and substantive benefits.

[c] Greater emphasis on achievement of substantive, ultimate goals and objective achievements.

- Measure the benefits or values using assessment indicators. One might subdivide the indicators into short-, mid-, and long-term ones based on the three stages described above (for example, Table A1).

Measure the costs and burdens, distinguishing between recurring and nonrecurring ones.

- Subdivide costs by category (labour, contract, materials, equipment distinguishing between hardware, software, and telecommunications). It is also useful to distinguish between fixed and variable costs, particularly if a charging scheme is needed. Even if their allocation is far from straightforward, overhead costs have to be considered.

- Identify sunk costs, if any, even though this may prove difficult. These costs cannot be recovered and should not be included in the cost streams.

- Project costs year-by-year for the life cycle of the project. Some costs may be the same each year, but others may change as the project matures. Such projections are sometimes referred to as "cost streams."

Step 5. Compare and evaluate alternatives

General comparison method: Using this approach, no attempt is made to express benefits and costs in terms of present value, estimate net present value, or compute a cost–benefit ratio. Evaluators simply scrutinize the supporting text and make their decision based on intuitive weighting (best, next best, etc.).

Present value method: With this approach, an attempt is made to express benefits and costs in terms of present value and net present value is calculated. The higher an alternative's net present value, the more its benefits exceed its costs.

Benefit–cost ratio method: Under this approach, the benefit–cost ratio is calculated by dividing the present value of benefits by that of costs. The ratio provides a relative measure of the benefits obtained per dollar spent and is particularly useful when comparing alternatives with unequal costs, benefits, and life cycles. This method does not allow comparison of the magnitude of the returns from several alternatives.

Step 6. Sensitivity analysis

Sensitivity analysis involves examining the assumptions of a CBA to determine their effects and influence on the final recommendations. For example, suppose our project will require five people to work in the computer room. Personnel costs are recurring over the life cycle of the project. Sensitivity analysis would be used to determine the effect on total costs of the system if the number of people required were reduced to two, three, or four. A possible trade-off might occur between more personnel (a recurring cost) and more expensive equipment (a one-time cost).

Step 7. Present results

The CBA should be presented, as far as possible, in a standardized manner. The findings should be organized in a familiar way and all important issues should be addressed. It is often useful to supplement the written report with oral briefings to allow the decision-makers to question the analysts, ask for clarification, amplification, etc.

Step 8. Select a preferred alternative

The CBA method does not "select" the preferred alternative. The decision is made by the policymaker or manager responsible for the project. It is based on information provided by the CBA as well as supplementary information obtained through independent research and counsel, oral briefings, and other third-party mechanisms. The final decision always depends on the judgment of the responsible official.

A Rural Community Resource Centre

————■————

The rural community resource centre or information centre represents a "bottom-up" approach that relies on the mobilization of resources at the rural level to meet information needs identified by members of the community. These resources include information materials, personnel, facilities, and funding as well as existing organizations.

An appropriate environment for demonstrating the benefits of providing access to information exists in rural areas of developing countries. The main economic activity here is primary production (agriculture or fishing), communities consist of 5 to 10 thousand people, and they exhibit marked cultural differences from the urban population based on tribal or other characteristics. It should be possible to identify direct and indirect benefits for each group with indicators that are expressed conceptually or empirically.

The hypothetical community is not using sophisticated information technology; computers and CD-ROM are not available and telecommunications links are unreliable. The information resources will consist of print and audiovisual material. In this type of environment, where the level of literacy is likely to be low, audiovisual material will be of great importance. Delivery of information will depend to a large extent on "change agents" (extension workers in agriculture, health, community development, sports, and other areas).

Benefits from the establishment of a rural community resource centre could accrue to three main constituencies: government agencies, communities (villages), and individuals. A tentative list of such benefits and the related expected results was compiled (Tables A2, A3, and A4).

Table A2. Benefits to government agencies.

Benefit	Result
Provide opportunity to identify more effectively and to meet the information needs defined by the community	Better supply of more appropriate information directed at rural communities More effective dissemination of information about government programs Increased willingness to participate in government programs
Facilitate the dissemination of rural development information by extension workers	Increased support for and participation in rural development projects
Provide feedback on community concerns and its reaction to plans and programs	Improvement in two-way communication between government agencies and local communities
Contribute to the preparation of well-informed citizens	Better informed decision-making at the community level

Table A3. Benefits to the community.

Benefit	Result
Provide information and activities that will enable community members to acquire skills	Increase in the variety of skills and jobs in community
Assist the community to acquire new knowledge	Increase in the understanding of and participation in community affairs and in effectiveness in handling them
Provide access to information about health, agricultural techniques, child care, nutrition, small businesses, etc.	Improvement in social and economic conditions
Strengthen communities' involvement and appreciation of local and national culture	Heightened awareness of national issues and greater national cohesiveness
Provide focal point for community activities	Increased cooperation and greater cohesiveness at community level
Encourage and facilitate the capture and storage of indigenous knowledge	Greater proporation of local information in the total knowledge base

Table A4. Benefits to the individual.

Benefit	Result
Locate and obtain information on subjects of interest	Broader knowledge base
Increase participation in learning activities	Acquisition of new skills and knowledge
Increase availability of and access to print and nonprint information resources	Retention of literacy and numeracy skills Greater access to information for illiterate people through oral or audiovisual resources
Provide opportunities for continuing education	Self-improvement and increased sense of self-worth
Recognize and use indigenous information based on the oral tradition	Increase in number of people willing to participate in programs designed to record indigenous knowledge

The groups receiving benefits might be defined more narrowly according to their interests, motivations, and roles in development. For example, an alternative classification would be government bureaucrats, local politicians, local leaders (nonpartisan), government extension workers, extension workers in nongovernmental organizations, members of community groups, citizens in general, and students.

Groups can be defined more precisely given sufficient background information about the constituencies served by the resource centre. Such characteristics as geographic location, size and structure of the population, main economic activities, and history of the location should be sought as well as information about the resources available at the centre (such as information products and services expected on a regular basis or on demand, size and quality of the staff, available technology such as computer, telecommunications, CD-ROM, etc.).

The change agent (extension worker) will also benefit from the centre, which will, in principle, provide an identifiable central store of information that the community can use. The extension worker can then determine precisely whether and what information is being consulted. The impact of the use of such information might be revealed in the behaviour of the members of the community.

Consider the hypothetical case of a health extension worker who supplies information on the benefits of child immunization. Indicators for resource centre staff could be the size and variety of information resources available in the centre and the number of times information is requested or consulted; the indicator for the health extension worker could be the response by the community in terms of number of children immunized compared with previous patterns.

Indicators to assess the degree to which the expected results are achieved must be identified and tested. For example, for the result "Increased participation in government programs," one could compare the percentage of people participating before and after implementation of the information program in their community. One must take care in formulating the indicators so that they relate as closely as possible to the information factor. A special survey would have to be carried out to ascertain the relative role of information and other inputs or incentives in the observed changes in participation. Otherwise, they may be erroneously attributed to information alone.

To assess accurately the impact of providing information, feedback should be obtained from people outside the information sector. The information provider can supply evidence of the number of times he or she was consulted, but not of the number of times the information was used. Information can only be said to have been used if related actions or perceptions can be observed.

To the extent that human intermediaries, whether professional or otherwise, are playing a key role in the operation of such services, benefits might be assessed by mapping, at successive times, their "information resources directory," both formal and informal. That is the memorized "addresses" of institutions, places, people, or documents, from which relevant information can be gathered. One can look at the breadth and depth of this map: how many sources are known for a given subject, how many characteristics of these sources are known, how often were they used.

The end users should also be considered regarding their actual use patterns and possible benefits from the information provided. The target community can be monitored, by observation and interviews at various times, to determine their "information resources directory," which information was actually obtained, what was used, and what was its effect on population characteristics, such as its information literacy and its well being.

An important indirect benefit of the use of a resource centre is the appropriation of the facility by the community. The community may now have the opportunity to control the flow of information — to gain self-determination in the provision of information. This may be observed at first in the formation of an advisory or governance board and its composition. The funding of the resource centre might provide another manifestation of this control in the ratio of public subsidies to community contributions and direct income. One might further observe the nature and rationale of management decisions. The local advisory board may, for instance, not only determine the level of staffing but also identify suitable personnel from within the community. It may also identify the nature of the information required and specify the products and services to be provided. This latter aspect may be cross-checked by observing, for example, the ratio of information material received without solicitation to material specifically requested.

Distinctions among the various types of benefits may be illustrated by the following example. Assume that a rural community resource centre maintains a register of the demand for information coming from the community. The immediate benefit for government officers in charge of satisfying the community's information needs would be increased knowledge (or reduced uncertainty) about the community's expressed information needs. A potential benefit would be opportunity to identify more effectively and to meet information needs as defined by the community. However, for this benefit to be fully realized would require further investigation of unexpressed information needs. A second, more remote potential benefit would be improved supply of more appropriate information to rural communities. For this to take place, many other favourable conditions must be met, such as the officers' drive to serve the community, willingness to make decisions, availability of facilities, and supportive management.

Appendix 4

CRITERIA OF THE US GOVERNMENT ACCOUNTING OFFICE

This Appendix presents the criteria that are used by the United States Government Accounting Office in assessing information activities.

Defining requirements

- What is the operational need being satisfied?

    1. Are the quantitative and qualitative deficiencies of the current information service or system real?

    2. Is the current system or service tied to a function for which there is a clear authority for the organization to perform?

    3. Are the deficiencies more organizational or operational than service or system related?

    4. Is the need tied to a specific decision that must be made or a specific report that must be developed?

    5. Does the service or system produce the information in a timely and useful fashion (does it have practical utility)?

- What impact does the system or service have?

    1. Does the system or service assure the quality of the data?

    2. Does the system or service achieve maximum throughput?

    3. Does the system or service contribute to better decisions by supplying necessary decision-linked data previously unavailable?

4. Does the system or service streamline or consolidate what would otherwise be disjointed functions or processes?

5. Is the system or service preventing an impending program failure or is it just alleviating or postponing one?

6. Are the impacts being realized now, or are they expected sometime in the distant future?

■ What are the objectives and the operational concept for the system or service?

1. Do the objectives of the system or service relate to the programmatic objectives of the organization? Is it tied to any higher level objectives?

2. Does the service or system blend into the programmatic functioning?

3. Does the service or system blend with other staff or user functions and activities?

4. To what extent would major or minor changes require modifications to the overall organization or operations?

5. If there are system or service changes, what specific program or system may result?

6. How many and what types of subsystems are there? Are they completely installed? If not, what is the schedule? Is it reasonable?

■ What are the performance levels of the system or service?

1. Do they meet or exceed the defined need?

2. What are the bounds of acceptability on these performance levels?

3. What is the chance of falling short of these levels? Impact of falling short?

4. Does the system or service perform at a consistent level, or is it in danger of degrading (saturation)?

■ For new development efforts, what is the required date for the system or service to become operational?

1. Is this date achievable based upon project schedules?

2. Is there sufficient control over tasks to ensure meeting this date?

3. Are the budgets and resources in place to ensure that the operational date is met?

4. Will the system or service be tested before it is declared operational?

5. Is there a backup capability if the operational date cannot be met?

Information systems or services planning and management

■ Have goals and objectives been identified and clearly stated?

1. Are the goals and objectives achievable?

2. Are the system goals and objectives limited to the programmatic goals and objectives?

3. Are they product oriented? Measurable?

■ Is accountability for costs and progress of the system or service development and operation assigned to specific individuals within the sponsoring organization?

1. Are these accountable individuals organizationally placed where they can control activities? Are they close enough to the activity to be aware of progress?

2. Is accountability established through formal certification of achievement of intermediate milestones?

3. Are there secondary and tertiary levels of accountability for integrating the efforts of suborganization activities toward achieving system or service development milestones?

4. Will a clear audit track exist that identifies and traces the sources of service or system development problems?

■ Are clear lines of authority established for making decisions affecting the system or service development?

1. Do these decision-making lines of authority correspond to the accountability network?

2. Are these decision-making lines of authority consistent with the organizational structure?

3. Can the decision-making process keep pace with established schedules?

■ Are tasks specific? Are they properly sequenced? Are assigned priorities adequately staffed?

■ Are schedules clearly defined with intermediate and accountable milestones to measure progress?

■ Are there contingency plans in place to handle budget funding interruptions, programmatic shifts, schedule slippages?

■ Are schedules clearly defined with intermediate and accountable milestones to measure progress?

■ Are resource requirements clearly specified and have steps to secure them been taken?

■ Do service or system development efforts conform to acceptable life-cycle management standards and guidelines?

System or service design

■ Does the system or service design recognize the fact that there may be an existing system or service in place which could be incorporated into the new design?

■ Does the designer allow for intermediate stages of sophistication or capability and plan modular growth to the final performance level?

■ Does the design rely on proven technology?

■ Does the design explicitly consider, and accommodate, the user as part of the system or service?

■ Does the system or service designer recognize necessary interfaces with other systems or services?

■ Will the design incorporate internal checks and balances?

■ Are alternatives being considered?

- Are security considerations and the use of standards explicit?
- Does the system or service provide for failure and "fail safe" contingencies?
- Does the design give proper consideration to the data?
    1. Are the data requirements clear and directly related to the use of the information?
    2. What controls are used to ensure the quality of the input data?
    3. What simplification, mechanization, or streamlining options can be introduced to reduce the labour intensity or increase the quality of data acquisition?

Applying the Assessment Framework

─────■─────

Among the case studies examined at the post-computer conference workshop, the one that received the most attention was Information for Decision-Making in the Caribbean Community (CARICOM). This project is designed to improve the effectiveness and sustainability of regional information systems and networks. In anticipation of the next phase of research — field-testing the impact assessment methods presented in this book — a small group of researchers, including the CARICOM project leader, took an in-depth look at how the assessment framework might be tested within the scope of this project. This case study is presented in three parts: the first provides an overview of the CARICOM project; the second looks at the feasibility of applying the assessment methods; and the third suggests what some of the outcomes and indicators might be.

Part 1. Overview of the project

Background

Information has been recognized as an important component of the regional development process in the Caribbean for more than 10 years and government commitment has been demonstrated, not only through mandates for the establishment of regional information systems, but also through the provision of facilities and the development of national information policies. Existing information systems in the Carribean cover the following sectors and issues:

- **Planning**: Caribbean Information System for Economic and Social Planning (CARISPLAN) and the Organization of Eastern Caribbean States' (OECS) infonet;

- **Trade**: Caribbean Trade Information System (CARTIS), the Eastern Caribbean States Export Development Agency (ECSEDA), and the Association of Caribbean Transformation–Agricultural Information System (ACT–AIS);

- **Energy**: the Caribbean Energy Information System (CEIS);

- **Policy research**: the documentation system of the Consortium Graduate School/Institute of Social and Economic Research (CGS/ISER);

- **Technology transfer**: the Caribbean Technological Consultancy Services (CTCS), the Caribbean Agricultural Research and Development Institute (CARDI), and the Caribbean Industrial Research Institute (CARIRI); and

- **Debt management**: the Commonwealth Secretariat–Debt Recording and Management System.

Regional information systems were evaluated (IDRC 1989). The major recommendations at that time were for greater integration of regional information systems; harmonization of mandates for establishing regional information networks; delivery of outputs and services in formats appropriate to the needs of development actors as users; optimizing existing facilities for human resources development in the management of information resources; incorporating compatible data structures to permit increased communication and data exchange between the regional networks; implementing mechanisms for facilitating information flows, particularly increased use of regional mass communication facilities for disseminating information about and from the regional networks; and establishing mechanisms for long-term sustainability of the regional information networks.

These findings were endorsed by the Conference of Heads of

Government of the Caribbean Community and the Caribbean Cooperation and Development Committee, who agreed to establish the Consultative Committee on Caribbean Regional Information Systems (CCCRIS) to monitor, advise on, and coordinate regional information systems and networks in the Caribbean. This committee prepared a plan for implementing the critical aspects of the strategy and the current project was developed to carry out a set of integrated activities to accomplish this.

Goal and objectives

The goal of the project is efficient management of information services for decision-makers and research and development actors in the Caribbean, and the provision of information products in a business-like and cost-effective manner tailored to identified regional needs.

The general objectives are

- To determine the optimal information services needed to support research and development activities in the Caribbean, in light of regional priorities, programs, and existing information systems;

- To carry out applied research and testing of methods for measuring, evaluating, and commercializing the services of the regional information systems and networks to ensure their sustainability;

- To improve communication among the information systems of regional sectors by establishing electronic interconnections to facilitate the delivery of interdisciplinary information; and

- To increase the capacity of regional information specialists in information resources management by strengthening the program of the School of Information Studies of the University of the West Indies (UWI).

The specific objectives are

- To identify and document the information needs and

information-seeking behaviour of selected strategic managers, professional technical personnel, and small business managers;

- To increase users' awareness of the regional information networks through promotional programs and further development of an integrated referral mechanism;

- To formulate and test guidelines for developing, pricing, and marketing information products and services;

- To research, formulate, and define criteria and assessment indicators for measuring performance, value, and efficiency of information services and products;

- To test performance criteria and assessment indicators for determining the impact of improved products and services of the information networks;

- To define a business strategy and marketing plan for use by the regional information networks including product development and testing;

- To identify constraints to commercialization of information as reflected in the policies of regional organizations and define required policy adjustments;

- To define and test a plan for developing capacity and increasing proficiency in information resources management in the region;

- To define a legal framework and guidelines for determining ownership of data and databases and for data collection, and investigate joint-venture opportunities among information suppliers and clients in information product development and marketing;

- To assess existing policies and constraints and identify instruments and actions required to improve intraregional data communication; and

- To develop guidelines for more effective data collection and access to the network databases.

Outputs

- A characterization of the target group, analyzing the information needs and information seeking behaviour of at least 100 regional development actors, and the development of a model for selective dissemination of information (SDI);

- An integrated referral mechanism guiding users to the information held by the regional information networks;

- A promotional program for the regional information networks implemented through the mass media;

- Tested guidelines for the development, pricing, and marketing of information products and services,

- Reports on performance criteria and assessment indicators of the impact of improved products and services of selected information networks; the impact of improved products and services of the information networks; a business strategy and marketing plan for the management of the regional networks; the constraints and policy adjustments required of the institutions coordinating the regional networks; regional training needs in the area of information resources management; guidelines for ownership of data and databases of cooperative networks and the feasibility of establishing joint ventures in information product development and marketing between a regional information network and a client; and policies, instruments and actions required to improve intra- and interregional data communication.

The reports will be used as tools in the management activities of the networks. They will be completed in the first 2 years of the project. However, ongoing monitoring by the organizations is expected, particularly with respect to the user study and the study of training needs to be carried out by the Department of Library Studies, UWI. A final report consolidating recommendations and proposals implemented during the project, as well as follow-up action required, will be prepared by the CARICOM Secretariat.

Users and beneficiaries

The project is expected to benefit

- Strategic managers, professional and technical people, and the managers of small businesses who will be participants in a model SDI service, and recipients of the improved products and services;

- Network managers and information professionals who will be exposed to new concepts in information resources management and receive guidelines for development and improvement of information products and services delivery and marketing;

- The UWI Department of Library Studies which will increase its institutional capacity to deliver programs in information management; and

- The CARICOM Secretariat and CCCRIS by improved information systems and networks and in their increased capacity to develop further the regional information networks.

Management and coordination

The CARICOM Secretariat, in undertaking the management and coordination of this project, will ensure integration of its activities around the coordinated development and use of the regional information networks, particularly the improved services and products to be provided within the SDI services model to the target group.

The Caribbean Community Secretariat, as the coordinator of CCCRIS, will be responsible for coordinating the activities of the project and for consolidating the individual reports for distribution to IDRC and the member institutions of CCCRIS.

Methods

The project consists of subprojects that are interconnected, so that the results of one provide input into subsequent activities, particularly to the ongoing SDI service, the human resources development component, and management and future development of the networks. Each subproject will be carried out and managed by one of the participating organizations.

All subprojects include preparation of a detailed work plan; evaluation of consultants' profiles and awarding of contracts; evaluation of consultant's reports. These activities will be the responsibility of the implementing agencies in consultation with the CARICOM Secretariat. All reports will be distributed to the managers of the networks and to the other members of the CCCRIS.

Research will be undertaken as a first activity of several of the subprojects. It will include

■ Identification of user needs and information-seeking habits;

■ Establishment of criteria for measuring performance, value and efficiency of information networks;

■ Development of a methodology for assessing the impact of improved products and services;

■ development of a business strategy and marketing plan for providing information services;

■ Curriculum and human resources development; and

■ Guidelines for the ownership of data and databases.

Testing as a means of verifying assumptions will be used wherever feasible and will be carried out in the following areas:

■ Products and services as an input into subprojects;

■ Performance and assessment criteria for use with information networks and methods for assessing the impact of information use;

■ Strategy for commercializing information networks;

■ Markets for selected information products; and

■ New procedures for data collecting and updating the databases.

In the absence of guidelines for certain types of operations and because of the need to clarify certain issues, the case studies will be documented and some operating principles deduced, for example in commercializing information products and services and in defining procedures for data collection.

Subproject I: User study and the provision of enhanced services from regional information networks — At least 100 strategic managers, professional and technical personnel, or managers of small businesses will be selected from institutions in all CARICOM states. The selection will be made from those institutions most suited to follow through with implementation.

SDI profiles will be prepared for each user, including an indication of their information-seeking habits and preference for packaging of information products and services. Adequate geographic and institutional sampling will be done to ensure a regional multiplier effect. In addition to providing services, this model will help determine the future of information network development in the region, as feedback received during the ongoing evaluation will be incorporated into the development of future services.

The CARICOM Secretariat will identify 40 strategic managers involved with the CARICOM regional development programs, both at the regional headquarters and in member states. Efforts will be made to identify people whose work would greatly benefit by the availability of critical information and who have influence with their colleagues. As a result of studies and analyses between 1988 and 1990, CARICOM is restructuring its institutions and has already established a Bureau of the Conference of Heads of Government that is, in effect, the executive arm of the Conference. It includes Decision Support Systems. The strategic managers will, thus, include decision-makers at the highest political levels.

The OECS Secretariat will identify 30 (or more) professional and technical people from within OECS, applying the same principle of ability to influence others both in the use of the information networks and in the support of the necessary information infrastructural developments.

The Caribbean Development Bank (CDB) and ISER will select 30 small business managers. For ISER, this activity is an extension of its Impact Assessment of the Information Sector (Jamaica) and fits into the continuum of research activity in this area as the university continues to be closely involved in regional development.

The CARICOM Secretariat will collaborate with the OECS Secretariat, and UWI and ISER in the selection process. Two consultants will be contracted by the CARICOM Secretariat to review the existing literature and prepare questionnaire(s) in a computerized format for analysis, to run sample tests, to administer questionnaires, and to interview the participants. The consultants will analyze responses and prepare user profiles; examine products and services offered by regional information networks and match them with the profiles; and prepare an analytical report to be used in the next stage to develop a business strategy and marketing plan.

This initial study is expected to result in a characterization of people from selected groups according to their information needs and information-seeking habits and preferred packaging for their information delivery services. It will include a report on the ability of existing regional information networks to satisfy the identified information needs. The report will be distributed to all the members of CCCRIS, the national coordinating centres, and national focal points.

Existing regional networks will then be evaluated to determine their ability to respond to the identified information needs. Feedback from the impact assessment, will allow them to make adjustments to ensure that the required products and services are provided to users during the project.

Subproject II: Business strategy and marketing plan — Manuals will be prepared to help information managers and specialists in the elaboration, pricing, and marketing of information products for selected users. Based on the CDB's experience in implementing its Caribbean Technology Consultancy Service and the experience of CARIRI with its Industrial Inquiry Information Service, the CDB will have primary responsibility for developing sample products and for preparing and disseminating the related manuals.

On the basis of the report from the user study, a consultant will prepare sample information products that will be tested on a subset of the target group and their effectiveness evaluated. Because we expect that there will be areas of common ground in the information-seeking habits of members of the target group, guidelines for product development will be aimed at specific groups.

Cost of products will be determined, then they will be packaged, priced, and test-marketed. Guidelines for pricing and marketing will be prepared, based on this pilot study and on the on-going experience of the CDB. The guidelines and manuals in various media will be distributed by the CDB to members of CCCRIS, to national coordinating centres, and to national focal points. Copies will also be sold through commercial channels. This experimental marketing activity is expected to provide a basis for determining the commercial feasibility of the services provided by the regional information networks.

Subproject III: Measurement of performance, efficiency, and value of information networks, services, and products — Planners and decision-makers in the information sector have been seeking objective criteria for planning and evaluating the performance of information networks and services; this concern has become more evident with organizational requirements for evaluating information services and because of the increased cost of information technology. Therefore, CCCRIS also aims to establish and test criteria and assessment indicators for measuring performance, value, and efficiency of the regional information networks and, at a broader level, to provide a basis for impact assessments in the information sector and for policy formulation.

A review of on-going research and of results relating to this problem will be carried out. This experience will be related to the services provided by regional information networks suitable criteria for the Caribbean will be determined. The IDRC-supported project, Assessment Indicators for the Impact of Information on Development, will provide an important basis for identifying relevant indicators. The international Federation for Information and Documentation (FID) may be invited to collaborate by identifying ongoing global research in this area.

The criteria will be tested in collaboration with selected regional information networks and recommendations for appropriate performance and assessment indicators, efficiency, and value criteria for the Caribbean will be made. This research, which will be undertaken by UWI's Consortium Graduate School for the Social Sciences, will provide the basis for indicators to be used in the next stage of the project.

Subproject IV: Development and testing of a method for impact assessment of improved products and services — Measuring the impact of products and services is a key element in planning for and establishing sustainable information networks. The project will examine existing methods to determine which are most appropriate. The assessment will be based on the use of the criteria and evaluation indicators defined earlier, and the test will be related to the new products resulting from the development of the business strategy and marketing plan. The target users will be the participants of the ongoing user study.

The impact of selected performance criteria, assessment indicators, and assumptions will be evaluated in relation to existing information networks: based on the user profiles, the regional networks' progress in providing improved services will be monitored; the impact of new products and services on a set of users will be measured; and the use of guidelines for commercialization of services will be monitored and evaluated.

CARDI and ISER will identify, in consultation with the CARICOM Secretariat and CDB, the improved information products to be assessed; select the subjects on whom the product impact is to be assessed; and define a method for undertaking the assessment. The method will be pretested on users. With the assistance of a consultant, it will be modified and finalized. CARDI and ISER will conduct the test on the selected users, analyze the data, and prepare a report, which will be distributed to all national and regional information networks for further testing and feedback.

Subproject V: Assessment of the potential for existing regional information networks to develop commercial services — To ensure the long-term sustainablility of regional information systems and the related national networks, CCCRIS has begun to explore possibilities for income generation by the networks. This subproject is designed to assess the potential and identify constraints (and the need to adjust policy) to the development of commercial services by existing regional information networks.

The OECS Secretariat will be responsible for this activity. In consultation with other network managers, it will produce guidelines for the operation of existing regional information networks as commercial ventures. The OECS will also undertake a feasibility study on establishing a regional information company to serve as a broker for the services offered by the regional networks. The viability of such a company will be examined and products and services will be tested in the marketplace.

Subproject VI: Increasing proficiency in the management of information and information resources in the region — The Department of Library Studies, UWI, will be responsible for this subproject to increase regional capacity to manage information and information resources and to provide and market cost-effective, efficient products and services. The work is expected to result in tested courses for Masters level and continuing education programs in information resources management and marketing.

During the project, a number of modules for these courses will be tested on 24 managers of national and regional information networks. In addition, the information needs of these managers will be determined, as will those of the region in general, and compared with the present curriculum of the Department of Library Studies. This will increase the Department's ability to respond to the needs of information users by providing training and continuing education for the type of networks and services needed to meet current and future demands. A database of information about regional information specialists, skills, and experience will be prepared by the Department of Library Studies as a by-product of the survey.

Wherever possible the resources of other UWI research and training institutions, such as the Caribbean Institute for Mass Communication and the Department of Management Studies, will be used to broaden the scope of the training offered.

The project will included support for training a cadre of information specialists equipped to respond more effectively to the changing needs of information users and to manage the kinds of systems and services necessary to meet current demands. A visiting professor will be contracted to review the curriculum at the Department of Library Studies and to assist in the definition of modules for modification of the current program. Two scholarships will be provided for training in library and information sciences and information materials related to the new subjects will be provided.

Subproject VII: Investigation of a legal framework for ownership of data and databases and development of guidelines for managing data collection and access — The issues involved in ownership of data and cooperative databases will be examined and the current situation, including the use of government data, in the Caribbean will be determined. The experience of the Trinidad and Tobago Ministry of Agriculture will serve as a case study. Recommendations regarding future developments in the Caribbean will be proposed.

CARTIS and CARISPLAN's data-collection experiences will be analyzed and strategies for data collection by government and nongovernmental bodies will be defined. Various methods for data collection will be tested and recommendations made. The results of these studies will have an impact on management of the regional information networks with regard to ownership of information and the possibility of marketing, commercialization, and long-term sustainability. The CARICOM Secretariat, the Economic Commission for Latin America and the Caribbean (ECLAC), and the UWI Department of Library Studies will collaborate in implementing this sub-project.

An investigation will be conducted into opportunities for a joint arrangement between information supplier and client to make widely available information that has been enhanced by the client's experience. Procedural guidelines for this type of arrangement will be prepared, subjected to external review, and finalized. The results will be made available to national and regional information networks and to the Department of Library Studies.

Subproject VIII: Extending information services through intraregional data communication and promotion of the services of the networks — As a follow-up to the Caribbean Computer-Based Communications project, which is currently being implemented by ECLAC, the aim of this subproject is to enhance user access to multidisciplinary information in the region through interconnection of existing information systems and to improve the flow of information among coordinators and managers of the various regional systems by exploiting existing electronic messaging systems. ECLAC will propose solutions to the problems of intraregional and intersystems data communication, including standards for the exchange of information as well as policies and policy instruments required.

ECLAC will hire a consultant to review the Computer-Based Communications project and study other initiatives in the telecommunications field to determine the policies, instruments, or agreements required to improve intraregional data communication. The consultant will also work with the relevant telecommunications administrations to develop a strategy for solving the problems identified.

ECLAC will extend access to its electronic data communication facilities to public libraries and other institutions that have not been able to participate in the previous project. Representatives from these institutions will be trained in the use of the e-mail and bulletin board services. The database of databases derived from the

Computer-Based Communication Project will be updated, expanded, and made available via the ECLAC bulletin board.

A program for publicizing availability and use of regional databases, products, and information services will be outlined by a public relations consultant, who will study the advantages and disadvantages of the existing programs in the Caribbean. The program and recommendations will be circulated to network managers in the Caribbean and to the members of CCCRIS for comment. The final program will be implemented by the participating organizations using the promotional materials prepared under the project.

Project review and evaluation

The project coordinator will set up a project management information network to monitor and report on the progress of the project. Each network manager will update their files concerning the project components monthly. The e-mail system will be used for ongoing discussions.

The project will be reviewed annually, to coincide with the workshops for network managers or with the annual meeting of the Association of Caribbean University and Research Libraries (ACURIL). The project review team will consist of the project coordinator, managers of subprojects, and the other members of CCCRIS. Semiannual meetings will also be held via the electronic bulletin board using the conferencing facility to allow for the participation of as many other information professionals and end-users as necessary and also via the Special Interest Group. The project coordinator will have face-to-face discussions with implementing agencies at least three times during the project. Final review and evaluation will take place in the 36th month of the project.

Ongoing evaluation will take place through the target group of the SDI service. Consultation with these users will provide regular feedback on the quality of the service, and the institutions will be able to improve products and services based on the guidelines provided in the business strategy and marketing plan.

Ongoing regional evaluation of the services will be carried out by CARICOM in consultation with UWI and the network managers. Measurement criteria established and pretested under subproject III will be used in this evaluation.

Evaluation of the training component will be done at two levels. The information managers participating in the workshops will be able to assess the value of the course and its potential for the management of the regional networks. In year 3 of the project, postgraduate students will be able to provide feedback on the usefulness of the course in the "real world."

Part 2. Applicability of the assessment methods

In June 1993, several of the participants in the computer conference and post-conference workshop conferred to see how the generic method of assessment developed at the workshop could be applied to the CARICOM project. To do this, the group

- Examined the objectives, methods, and context of the CARICOM project, making direct linkages to concepts contained in the outputs of the post-conference workshop (such as IUEs, target audiences for indicators, expected benefits, outcomes vis-à-vis impact, and causality between information and impact);

- Reviewed the method for developing indicators that was produced during the workshop to clarify understanding of the terminology, check on the logic of the sequential steps, highlight major components requiring particular attention, and flag conspicuous parallels and entry points for the CARICOM project;

- Adapted the basic method to suit the specific requirements of the CARICOM project;

- Discussed examples of benefits and indicators that would probably be of relevance in the CARICOM project; and

- Applied the method to the specific circumstances of the CARICOM project, listing actions to be taken and a timetable.

This preliminary analysis confirmed that the basic assessment framework could be applied to the CARICOM project with only minor modifications. These modifications related mainly to the sequence of steps believed to be appropriate for this project. The four basic building blocks of the assessment framework were found to be readily applicable: identifying and describing the users, understanding the development problems and expected benefits, measuring inputs and outputs of the information system, and communicating the findings to the right target audiences.

The specific components of the method to be applied within the CARICOM project are listed below. It is interesting to compare this list with the generic one in Chapter 6.

- Define user communities.

- Describe the IUEs of the user communities.

- Define the target audiences for the assessment results (senior policymakers, information managers, professional and technical users, donors, general public).

- Determine the information life cycle (from the perspective of users and information managers).

- Set up standard guidelines for collecting, analyzing, and interpreting data, including anecdotes.

- Design and pretest survey questionnaire (pretesting checks for ability to categorize responses, such as individual measures of satisfaction).

- Undertake a baseline survey, which must be able to accommodate data and anecdotes; the latter should also be converted for use in the structured analysis, as well as providing illustrative material for use in presentations.

- Assemble baseline data.

- Define the declared objectives of the development program for which information is needed.

- Analyze survey findings to identify primary objectives and specific types of benefits expected by users.

- Develop a hierarchy of objectives or outcomes, grouping them into the various categories of benefits.

- Identify outputs in relation to outcomes or benefits to maximize effectiveness.

- Establish input requirements to deliver these outputs, using the matrix drafted at the workshop.

- Specify other factors that influence outcomes, positively or negatively.

- Identify critical factors that are information-dependent or informational in nature.

- Identify and define the indicators, drawing upon the categories that have been proposed.

- Continue periodic data collection.

- Analyze findings and categorize them.

- Aggregate and describe individual instances of indicators.

- Repackage for presentation to key target audiences.

- Obtain feedback.

The CARICOM project was officially launched in June 1993. The first steps will involve getting organized to be able to manage data collection, designing and pretesting the survey questionnaire of information managers and users, and preparatory work on potential indicators. With these initial measures accomplished along with compilation of baseline data, a seminar will be held late in 1993 to sensitize several information managers to the method and their role in its implementation over the 3 years of the project.

Part 3. Examples of benefits and indicators

Discussions about the CARICOM project at the post-conference workshop and later were exploratory. No attempt was made to identify definitive measures of input and output, types of benefits, or derived indicators. Nevertheless, the conversations did point to areas of benefit, likely indicators, and other illustrative examples.

In defining the user communities for the regional information systems encompassed by the CARICOM project, we expected that focus would be on three main categories:

- Policymakers and strategic managers,

- Professional and technical staff in various sectors, and

- The small business community.

Within each of these, the user survey would identify intended benefits in each of the proposed categories (political, economic, social, cultural, and technological). For example, positive outcomes of trade information systems could include entrepreneurs becoming more aware of and gaining access to external markets leading to increased sales, production, and employment, with associated economic and social benefits. In the public sector, better information about the extent of external debt and scenarios for its management would strengthen the negotiating position of finance officials, possibly leading to more favourable terms. In the agricultural research community, effective access to knowledge about new plant-culture techniques or pest management could save time and money in developing local methods for improving agricultural productivity for domestic consumption and export. Hopefully, the initial project survey would encourage users to identify such specific benefits, which could then be monitored periodically to measure the extent to which they had been achieved.

Permutations of this kind of data on usage and outcomes, together with information about specific inputs and outputs, will lead to derived measures or indicators. A preliminary look at the scope of the CARICOM project suggested that the indicators eventually developed might include some of the following:

Performance indicators

- Cost per unit output,

- Productivity,

- Efficiency,
- Cost per attribute level,
- Productivity by attribute level, and
- Economies of scale.

Effectiveness indicators

- Importance of services,
- Satisfaction with attributes,
- Amount of use of services,
- Number of referrals, and
- Ease of use of services (for example, user time spent).

Impact indicators (related to consequences of use)

- Time saved (user time) — by service or by information;
- Improved decision-making, research, planning, analysis; cooperation, etc., in terms of quality, timeliness, and so on;
- Return on investment for the user, the organization, or the community, in terms of service or information;
- Opportunity costs (nonusers) (cost of lost benefits);
- Needs met or unmet by the service;
- Use per capita in target population;
- Number of users in target population (market penetration); and
- Awareness of target population.

This initial exploration suggests that the method developed during the workshop does indeed provide a feasible approach for assessing the impact of information systems in the Caribbean. The field-testing that is now taking place will confirm the extent to which the generic assessment model proves applicable, and whether any refinements are necessary.

ACRONYMS AND ABBREVIATIONS

———— ■ ————

ACT–AIS   Association of Caribbean Transformation–Agricultural Information System

ASIS   American Society for Information Science

CARDI   Caribbean Agricultural Research and Development Institute

CARIRI   Caribbean Industrial Research Institute

CARISPLAN   Caribbean Information System for Economic and Social Planning

CARTIS   Caribbean Trade Information System

CBA   cost–benefit analysis

CCCRIS   Consultative Committee on Caribbean Regional Information Systems

CDB   Caribbean Development Bank

CDCC   Caribbean Cooperation and Development Committee

CEIS   Caribbean Energy Information System

CGS   Consortium Graduate School, Univeristy of the West Indies

CPR   Common Pool Resources [model]

CS–DRMS	Commonwealth Secretariat–Debt Recording and Management System
CTCS	Caribbean Technological Consultancy Services
ECLAC	Economic Commission for Latin America and the Caribbean
ECSEDA	Eastern Caribbean States Export Development Agency
FID	International Federation for Documentation
GNP	gross national product
IDRC	International Development Research Centre
IRM	information resources management
ISER	Institute of Social and Economic Research
IUE	information use environment
OECS	Organization of Eastern Caribbean States
ORM	Organization Resource Management [model]
SCIP	Society of Competitive Intelligence Professionals
SDI	selective dissemination of information
UNDP	United Nations Development Programme
UNRISD	United Nations Research Institute for Social Development
UWI	University of the West Indies

BIBLIOGRAPHY

———————■———————

This bibliography includes all citations specifically referred to in the book, publications referred to and used during the computer conference but not specifically cited here, as well as further readings on the subjects of assessing the impact of information and computer conferencing.

Agha, S.S. 1992. Sustainability of information systems in developing countries: an appraisal and suggested courses of action. International Development Research Centre, Ottawa, ON, Canada. IDRC-MR316e.

Agha, S.S.; Akhtar, S. 1992. The responsibility and the response: sustaining information systems in developing countries. Journal of Information Sciences, 18, 283–292.

Aiyepeku, W.O. 1989. The perception and utilization of information by policy-makers in Nigeria. National Library of Nigeria, Lagos, Nigeria.

_____ 1993. Integrative and value-added properties of information in space and time. Presented at the International Conference on West-African Integration, Dakar, Senegal. Economic Community of West African States, Dakar, Senegal.

Allen, T.J. 1964. The utilization of information sources during R&D proposal preparation. MIT Press, Cambridge, MA, USA. Alfred P. Sloan School of Management Working Paper No. 97-64.

_____ 1970. Roles in technical communications networks. In Nelson, C.E.; Pollock, D.K., ed., Communication among scientists and engineers. Heath Lexington Books, Lexington, MA, USA.

Annerstedt, J.; Jamieson, A., ed. 1988. From research policy to social intelligence. Macmillan, London, UK. Essays for Stevan Dedijer.

Anonymous. 1992. Infoterra success stories 1991. Infoterra Bulletin, 14(2), 4–5.

ARL (Association of Research Libraries). 1988. User surveys. ARL, Office of Management Services, Washington, DC, USA. Spec Kit No. 148.

Baumol, W.J.; Braunstein, Y.M.; Fisher, D.M.; Ordover, J.D. 1981. Manual of pricing and cost determination for organizations engaged in dissemination of knowledge. New York University, New York, NY, USA.

Bezanson, K. 1992. Expanded mandate for IDRC. International Development Research Centre, Ottawa, ON, Canada.

Bickner, R.E. 1983. Concepts of economic cost. In King, D.W.; Roderer, N.K.; Olsen, H.A., ed., Key papers in the economics of information. Knowledge Industry Publications, White Plains, NY, USA. pp. 107–146.

Bookstein, A. 1981. An economic model of library service. Library Quarterly, 51(4), 410–428.

Boon, J.A. 1992. Information and development: towards an understanding of the relationship. South African Journal of Library and Information Science, 60(2), 63–74.

Borko, H.; Menou, M.J. 1983. Index of information utilization potential (I.U.P.). United Nations Educational, Scientific and Cultural Organisation, Paris, France. Serial No. PGI-1-83/WS/29. 114 pp.

Boulding, K.E. 1966. The economics of knowledge and the knowledge of economics. American Economic Review, 56(2), 1–13.

Braunstein, Y.M. 1985. Information as a factor of production: substitutability and productivity. Information Society, 3(3), 261–273.

_____ 1989. Library funding and economics: a framework for research. IFLA Journal, 15, 289–297.

Brinberg, H.R. 1982. The contribution of information to economic growth and development. In Ammundsen, V., ed., Organization and economics of information and documentation. Proceedings of the 40th FID Congress. International Federation for Documentation, The Hague, Netherlands.

Broadbent, M. 1992. Demonstrating information service value to your organization. In Raitt, D.I., ed., Online information 92: 16th international online information meeting proceedings. Learned Information, Oxford, UK. pp. 65–84.

Buckland, M.K. 1982. Concepts of library goodness. Canadian Library Journal, 39(2), 63–66.

Byrd, G.D. 1989. The economic value of information. Law Library Journal, 81(2), 191–201.

Carbo Bearman, T. 1988. Uses of scientific, technical and societal information by policy makers. Knowledge in Society, 1988(Spring), 27–53.

_____ 1992. Information transforming society: challenges for the year 2000. Information Services and Use, 12, 217–223.

Casper, C.A. 1983. Economics and information science. In Debons, A., ed., Information science in action: system design. Martinus Nijhoff Publishers, London, UK.

Cawkell, A.E. 1984. Economics of the information society. Journal of Information Science, 8(1), 42–44.

_____ 1989. The risks of ignoring information. Information Services and Use, 9, 325–326.

Chick, M. 1989. Information value and cost measures for use as management tools. Presented at the state-of-the-art institute, 6–8 November 1989, Washington, DC. Special Libraries Association, Washington, DC, USA.

Cochrane, G.; Atherton, P. 1980. The cultural appraisal of efforts to alleviate information inequity. Journal of the American Society for Information Science, 31(4), 283–292.

Coombs, P.H.; Hallak, J. 1987. Cost analysis in education, a tool for policy and planning. Johns Hopkins University Press, Baltimore, MD, USA.

Cooper, M.N. 1983. The structure and future of the information economy. Information Processing and Management, 19(1), 9–16.

Copley, J. 1989. As you sow, so shall you reap: understanding the value of information. Aslib Proceedings, 4(11/12), 319–329.

Cronin, B. 1981. Assessing user needs. Aslib Proceedings, 33(2), 37–47.

_____ 1986. Towards information-based economics. Journal of Information Science, 12, 129–137.

Cronin, B.; Gudim, M. 1986. Information and productivity: a review of research. International Journal of Information Management, 6(2), 85–101.

Cronin, M.J. 1985. Performance measurement for public services in academic and research libraries. Association of Research Libraries, Office of Management Studies, Washington, DC, USA. Occasional Paper No. 9.

Davenport, E. 1992. A methodology for exploring electronic scholarship. *In* Raitt, D.I., ed., Online information 92: 16th international online information meeting proceedings. Learned Information, Oxford, UK. pp. 15–24.

Dedijer, S.; Jequier, N. 1988. Intelligence for economic development. Macmillan, London, UK.

Dervin, B. 1977. Useful theory for librarianship: communication, not information. Drexel Library Quarterly, 13(3), 16–32.

_____ 1983a. Information as a user construct: the relevance of perceived information needs to synthesis and interpretation. *In* Ward, S.A.; Reed, L.J., ed., Knowledge structures and use: implications for synthesis and interpretation. Temple University Press, Philadelphia, PA, USA. pp. 153–184.

_____ 1983b. An overview of sense-making: concepts, methods, and results to date. Paper presented at the International Association Annual Meeting, May 1983, Dallas, TX, USA.

_____ 1984. The information needs of Californians. Institute of Governmental Affairs, University of California at Davis, Davis, CA, USA. Report No. 2.

Dervin, B.; Dewdney, P. 1986. Neutral questioning: a new approach to the reference interview. RQ, 25(4), 506–513.

Dervin, B.; Jacobson, T.L.; Nilan, M.S. 1982. Measuring aspects of information seeking: a test of a quantitative/qualitative methodology. *In* Burgoon, M., ed., Communication yearbook, vol. 6. Sage Publications, Beverly Hills, CA, USA. pp. 419–444.

Dervin, B.; Nilan, M.S. 1984. Information needs and uses. Annual Review of Information Science and Technology, 21, 3–33.

Dizard, W. 1982. The coming of information age: an overview of technology, economics and politics. Longmans, New York, NY, USA.

Doctor, R.D. 1992. Social equity and information technologies: moving toward information democracy. Annual Review of Information Science and Technology, 27, 43–96.

Doll, R. 1981. Information technology and its socio-economic and academic impact. Online Review, 5(1), 37–46.

Edelstein, A.S.; Bowes, J.E.; Harsel, S.W., ed. 1978. Information societies: comparing the Japanese and American experiences. International Communications Centre, University of Washington, Seattle WA, USA.

El Sherif, H. 1990. Managing institutionalization of strategic decision support for the Egyptian cabinet. Interfaces, 20(1), 97–114.

El Sherif, H.; El Sawy, O.A. 1988. Issue-based decision support systems for the Egyptian cabinet. MIS Quarterly, 12(4), 551–569.

Ernst, D.; O'Connor, D. 1990. Technology and global competition: the challenge for newly industrializing economies. Organisation for Economic Co-operation and Development, Paris, France.

Feldman, M.S.; March, J.G. 1981. Information in organizations as sign and symbol. Administrative Science Quarterly, 26, 171–186.

Feltham, G.A. 1968. The value of information. Accounting Review, 43(4), 684–696.

Flowerdew, A.D.J.; Oldman, C.M.; Whitehead, C.M.E. 1984. The pricing and provision of information. British Library, London, UK.

Flowerdew, A.D.J.; Whitehead, C.M.E. 1974. Cost-effectiveness and cost/benefit analysis in information science. London School of Economics and Political Science, London, UK. QSTI Report No. 5206.

Frants, V.I.; Brush, C.B. 1988. The need for information and some aspects of information retrieval systems construction. Journal of the American Society for Information Science, 39(2), 86–91.

Fray, C.P. 1978. The high cost of non-information. Jamaica Journal, 11(3/4), 50–53.

Garvey, W.D.; Tomita, K.; Woolf, P. 1979. The dynamic scientific information user. In Garvey, W.D., ed., Communication: the essence of science. Pergamon Press, Elmsford, NY, USA. pp. 256–279.

Gathegi, J.N. 1992. The state and society: intervention in the creation of scientific information in developing countries. Journal of the American Society for Information Science, 43(4), 323–333.

Girt, J.L. 1979. A measure of quality opportunity. Social Indicators Research, 6, 91–102.

Griffiths, J.M. 1982. The value of information and related systems, products and services. Annual Review of Information Science and Technology, 17, 269–284.

Griffiths, J.M.; King, D.W. 1986. The contribution of online database services to the productivity of their users. In Proceedings, 69–76. Learned Information, Medford, NJ, USA.

_____ 1990. Keys to success: performance indicators for public libraries. HMSO Office of Arts and Libraries, London, UK. Library Information Series No. 18.

_____ 1991. A manual on the evaluation of information centers and services. North Atlantic Treaty Organization, Neuilly sur Seine, France.

_____ 1993. Special libraries: increasing the information edge. Special Libraries Association, Washington, DC, USA.

Hamburg, M.; Clelland, R.C.; Bommer, M.R.W.; Ramist, L.E.; Whitfield, R.M. 1974. Library planning and decision making systems. MIT Press, Cambridge, MA, USA.

Hanson, J.; Narula, U. 1990. New communication technologies in developing countries. Lawrence Erlbaum Associates, Hillsdale, NJ, USA.

Harmon, G. 1984. The measurement of information. Information Processing and Management, 20(1/2), 193–198.

Harmon, P.; King, D. 1985. Expert systems: artificial intelligence in business. John Wiley & Sons, New York, NY, USA.

Hastedt, G. 1991. Intelligence and US foreign policy: how to measure success? International Journal of Intelligence and Counterintelligence, 5(1), 49–62.

Hayes, R.M., ed. 1985. Libraries and the information economy of California: a conference sponsored by the California State Library. Graduate School of Library and Information Science, University of California at Los Angeles, Los Angeles, CA, USA.

_____ 1992. Development of business plans in an information-based, market-oriented economy. In Cronin, B.; Tudor-Silovic, N., ed., From information management to social intelligence: the key to open markets. Aslib, London, UK. pp. 77–94.

Hayes, R.M.; Becker, J. 1984. Cost accounting in libraries. In Costing and the economics of library and information services. Aslib, London, UK. pp. 7–25.

Hayes, R.M.; Pollack, A.M.; Nordhaus, S. 1983. An application of the Cobb-Douglas model to the Association of Research Libraries. Library and Information Science Research, 5(3), 291–325.

Hayes, R.M.; Erickson, T. 1982. Added value as a federal function of purchases of information services. Information Society, 1(4), 307–339.

Hewins, E.T. 1990. Information need and use studies. Annual Review of Information Science and Technology, 25, 145–172.

Hicks, N.; Streeten, P. 1979. Indicators of development: the search for a basic yardstick. World Development, 7, 567–580.

Hilton, R.W. 1981. The determinants of information value: synthesizing some general results. Management Science, 27(1), 57–64.

Hirschleifer, J. 1973. Economics of information: where are we in the theory of information? American Economic Review, 63(2), 31–39.

Horton, F.W., Jr. 1979. Information resources management: concept and cases. Association for Systems Management, Cleveland, OH, USA.

——— 1983. Information literacy versus computer literacy. Bulletin of the American Society for Information Science, 9(4), 14–16.

——— 1984. The public-private sector controversy over disseminating government information. Journal of Public Communication, 6(1), 21–25.

Horton, F.W., Jr; Lewis, D. 1991. Great information disasters. Aslib, London, UK.

Horowitz, I.L. 1979. Methods and strategies in evaluating equity research. Social Indicators Research, 6, 1–22.

IDRC (International Development Research Centre). 1989. A regional information system strategy for the Caribbean for the year 2000. IDRC, Ottawa, ON, Canada. IDRC-MR214e.

——— 1990. The global research agenda: a North–South perspective. IDRC, Ottawa, ON, Canada.

——— 1991. Empowerment through knowledge: the strategy of the International Development Research Centre. IDRC, Ottawa, ON, Canada.

Imboden, N. 1978. A management approach to project appraisal and evaluation with special reference to non-directly producing projects. Organisation for Economic Co-operation and Development, Paris, France.

Jeong, D.Y. 1990. The nature of the information sector in the information society: an economic and social perspective. Special Libraries, 81(3), 175–179.

Jonscher, C. 1983. Information resources and economic productivity. Information Economics and Policy, 1(1), 13–35.

Jungk, R. 1969. Imagination and the future. International Social Sciences Journal, 21(4), 560.

Jussawalla, M.; Lamberton, D.M., ed. 1982. Communication economics and development. Pergamon Press, Elmsford, NY, USA.

Jussawalla, M.; Lamberton, D.M.; Karunaratne, N.D., ed. 1988. The cost of thinking: information economies in ten Pacific countries. Ablex Publishing, Norwood, NJ, USA.

Jussawalla, M.; Okuma, T.; Araki, T., ed. 1989. Information technology and global interdependence. Greenwood Press, New York, NY, USA.

Kantor, P.B. 1976. Availability analysis. Journal of the American Society for Information Science, 27, 31.

———— 1981. The present and future of cost studies: what good do they do? *In* Challenges to an information society: proceedings of the 47th ASIS annual meeting. Knowledge Industry Publications, White Plains, New York, USA.

———— 1989. Library cost analysis. Library Trends, 38, 171–188.

King, D.N. 1987. The contribution of hospital library information services to clinical care: study in eight hospitals. Bulletin of the Medical Library Association, 75(4), 291–301.

King, D.W., ed. 1978. Key papers in the design and evaluation of information systems. Knowledge Industry Publications, White Plains, NY, USA.

King, D.W.; Griffiths, J.M.; Roderer, N.K.; Wiederkehr, R.R.V. 1982. Value of the energy data base. Technical Information Center, United States Department of Energy, Oak Ridge, TN, USA.

King, D.W.; Griffiths, J.M.; Sweet, E.A.; Wiederkehr, R.R.V. 1984. A study of the value of information and the effect on value of intermediary organizations, timeliness of services and products, and comprehensiveness of the EDB. Volume 1. The value of libraries as an intermediary information service. Office of Science and Technical Information, United States Department of Energy, Oak Ridge, TN, USA. DOE/NBM-1078 (DE 85003670).

King, D.W.; McDonald, D.D.; Roeckrer, N.K.; Wood, B.L. 1976. Statistical indicators of scientific and technical communication (1960–1980). Vol. 1. A summary report. US Government Printing Office, Washington, DC, USA.

King, D.W.; Roderer, N.K. 1979. Information transfer cost/benefit analysis. *In* Information and industry: proceedings of the North Atlantic Treaty Organization, Advisory Group for Aerospace Research and Development (AGARD), Technical Information Panel's specialists' meeting, 18–19 October 1979, Paris, France. AGARD, Neuilly-sur-Seine, France.

King, D.W.; Roderer, N.K.; Olsen, H.A., ed. 1983. Key papers in the economics of information. Knowledge Industry Publications, White Plains, NY, USA.

King, W.R.; Epstein, B.J. 1976. Assessing the value of information. Management Datamatics, 5(4), 171–180.

Klitgaard, R. 1991. Adjusting to reality: beyond "state versus market" in economic development. ICS Press, San Francisco, CA, USA.

Kochen, M. 1983. Information and society. Annual Review of Information Science and Technology, 18, 277–304.

Koenig, M.E.D. 1982. Determinants of expert judgement of research performance. Scientometrics, 4(5), 361–378.

_____ 1990. Information services and downstream productivity. Annual Review of Information Science and Technology, 25, 55–86.

Koenig, M.E.D.; Kerson, L. 1983. Strategic and long range planning in libraries and information centers. In McCabe, G.B.; Kreissmin, B., ed., Advances in library administration and organization, vol. 2. JAI Press, Greenwich, CT, USA. pp. 199–258.

Korten, D.C. 1986. Strategic organization for people-centered development. In Ickis, J.C.; de Jesus, E.; Maru, R., ed., Beyond bureaucracy: strategic management of social development. Kumarian Press, West Hartford, CT, USA.

Krevitt-Eres, B. 1982. Socio-economic conditions relating to the level of information activity in less developed countries. Drexel University, Philadelphia, PA, USA. PhD dissertation.

Krevitt-Eres, B.; Lunin, L., ed. 1985. Perspectives on international information issues. Journal of the American Society for Information Science, 36(3), 144–199.

Lamberton, D.M., ed. 1971. Economics of information and knowledge: selected readings. Penguin Books, Harmondsworth, UK.

_____ 1984. The economics of information and organization. Annual Review of Information Science and Technology, 19, 3–30.

Lancaster, F.W. 1971. The cost-effectiveness analysis of information retrieval and dissemination systems. Journal of the American Society for Information Science, 22, 12–27.

_____ 1977. The measurement and evaluation of library services. Information Resources Press, Washington, DC, USA.

_____ 1979. Information retrieval systems: characteristics, testing and evaluation (2nd ed.). John Wiley and Sons, New York, NY, USA.

Lau, J. 1988. A study of selected social factors influencing information development in low, middle and highly developed countries: an assessment for the period 1960–1977. University of Sheffield, Sheffield, UK. PhD dissertation.

Lecomte, B.J. 1986. Project aid: limitations and alternatives. Organisation for Economic Co-operation and Development, Paris, France.

Logelin, M. 1992. Information et développement: étude synthétique des lignes de force du discours universitaire. Institut Universitaire de Technologie B, Département Carrières de l'Information et de la Communication, Université de Bordeaux, Bordeaux, France. Mémoire de DUT.

Machlup, F. 1962. The production and distribution of knowledge in the United States. Princeton University Press, Princeton, NJ, USA.

_____ 1979. Uses, value and benefits of knowledge. Knowledge: Creation, Diffusion, Utilization, 1(1), 62–81.

_____ 1980a. Knowledge: its creation, distribution and economic significance. Volume 1. Knowledge and knowledge production. Princeton University Press, Princeton NJ, USA.

_____ 1980b. Knowledge: its creation, distribution and economic significance. Volume 2. The branches of learning. Princeton University Press, Princeton NJ, USA.

Mackenzie-Owen, J.S. 1992. Waarde-apecten van informatie-verzorging. [Aspects of the value of information.] RABIN, The Hague, Netherlands.

Magrill, R.M. 1985. Evaluation by type of library. Library Trends, 33, 267–295.

Marschak, J. 1968. Economics of inquiring, communicating, deciding. American Economic Review, 58(2), 1–18.

Martin, F.S. 1989. Common pool resources and collective action: a bibliography. In Workshop in political theory and policy analysis. Indiana University, Bloomington, IN, USA.

Martyn, J. 1980. Library and information services provided to local government officials and others in Leicestershire: a study of costs and benefits. Aslib, London, UK. Aslib Research Report No. 1.

_____ 1986. Literature searching habits and attitudes of research scientists. The Research Group, London, UK.

Martyn, J.; Cronin, B. 1983. Assessing the impact and benefits of information and library research. Journal of Chemical Education, 39, 171–191.

Martyn, J.; Flowerdew, A.D.J. 1983. The economics of information. The British Library Board, London, UK.

Martyn, J.; Lancaster, W.E. 1981. Investigative methods in library and information science: an introduction. Information Resources Press, Arlington VA, USA.

Maruyama, M. 1974. Endogenous research vs. delusions of relevance and expertise among exogenous academics. Human Organization, 33, 318–322.

Maslow, A.H. 1968. Toward a psychology of being (2nd ed.). Van Nostrand Reinhold, New York, NY, USA.

Mason, R.M. 1979. A study of the perceived benefits of information analysis center services. Metrics Inc., Atlanta, GA, USA.

Mason, R.M.; Sassone, P.G. 1978. A lower bound cost benefit model for information services. Information Processing and Management, 14(2), 71–83.

Matarazzo, J.M.; Prusak, L.; Gauthier, M.R. 1990. Valuing corporate libraries: a survey of senior managers. Temple, Barker and Sloane Inc., Washington, DC, USA.

McClure, C.R. 1986. A view from the trenches: costing and performance measures for academic library public services. College and Research Libraries, 47, 323–336.

Mchombu, K. 1991. Information provision for rural development: a final report of phase one of the INFORD research project. Department of Library and Information Studies, University of Botswana, Gaborone, Botswana.

Menou, M.J. 1983. Cultural barriers to the international transfer of information. Information Processing and Management, 19(3), 121–129.

_____ 1985. An overview of social measures of information. Journal of the American Society for Information Science, 36(3), 169–177.

_____ 1989. L'information troisième frontière du développement?" In Sorieul, F., ed., L'information pour le développement en Afrique. Afrique contemporaine, No. 151, pp. 22–36.

_____ 1991. National information policy in the less developed countries: an educational perspective. International Library Review, 23(1), 49–64.

Michel, J. 1990. VAID — value analysis applied to information and documentation services and products. IATUL Quarterly, 4(2), 82–89.

Miles, I. 1990. Mapping and measuring the information economy. Research and Development Department, British Library, London, UK. Library and Information Research Report No. 77.

Morris, D.M. 1979. Measuring the condition of the world's poor. Pergamon Press, Elmsford, NY, USA.

Morrisson, C. 1989. The impact of development projects on poverty. Organisation for Economic Co-operation and Development, Paris, France.

Mulroney, B. 1992. IDRC: an Agenda 21 organization. Notes for an address to the Earth Summit, June 1992, Rio de Janeiro, Brazil. Government of Canada, Ottawa, ON, Canada.

NLM (National Library of Medicine). 1988. Survey of individual users of MEDLINE on the NLM system. NLM, Bethesda, MD, USA. NTIS: PB89-133722.

Neelameghan, A. 1981. Some issues in information transfer: a Third World perspective. IFLA Journal, 7(1), 8–18.

OECD (Organisation for Economic Co-peration and Development). 1978. Impact on employment, growth and trade. In Information activities, electronics and telecommunications technologies, vol. 1. OECD, Paris, France.

_____ 1986. New information technologies: a challenge for education. OECD, Paris, France.

_____ 1988. Evaluation in developing countries: a step in a dialogue. OECD, Paris, France.

_____ 1990. Public management development survey 1990. OECD, Paris, France.

_____ 1991. Development co-operation: efforts and policies of the members of the development assistance committee (1991 report). OECD, Paris, France.

_____ 1992. Adult illiteracy and economic performance. OECD, Paris, France.

Orpen, C. 1985. The effect of managerial distribution of scientific and technical information on company performance. R&D Management, 15(4), 305–308.

Orr, R.H. 1973. Measuring the goodness of library services: a general framework for considering quantitative measures. Journal of Documentation, 29, 314–332.

Ostrom, E. 1990. Governing the commons: the evolution of institutions for collective action. Cambridge University Press, Cambridge, UK.

Paisley, W. 1980. Information and work. *In* Dervin, B., Voigt, M., ed., Progress in communication sciences, vol. 2. Ablex Publishing, Norwood, NJ. pp. 113–166.

———— 1985. Rithms of the future: learning and working in the age of algorithms. *In* Hayes, R.M., ed., Libraries and the information economy of California: a conference sponsored by the California State Library. University of California at Los Angeles, Los Angeles, CA, USA. pp. 159–227.

Palvia, P.; Palvia, S.; Zigli, R.M. 1990. Models and requirements for using strategic information systems in developing nations. International Journal of Information Management, 10, 117–126.

Pinelli, T.E.; Glassman, M. 1989. An evaluation of selected NASA scientific and technical information products: result of a pilot study. National Aeronautics and Space Administration, Washington, DC, USA. TM101533.

Poats, R.M. 1986. Development cooperation: 25 years of development cooperation efforts and policies of the members of the Development Assistance Committee. Organisation for Economic Co-operation and Development, Paris, France.

Poliniere, J.P. 1974. Using and improving national information systems for development: some practical implications for policy-makers. United Nations Educational, Scientific and Cultural Organisation, Paris, France. Serial SC/74/WS/53.

Porat, M.V.; Rubin, M. 1977. The information economy: definition and measurements. Office of Telecommunications, US Department of Commerce, Washington, DC, USA. OT Special Publication 77-12, vol. 1.

Repo, A.J. 1986a. Analysis of the value of information: a study of some approaches taken in the literature of economics, accounting and management science. University of Sheffield, Sheffield, UK.

———— 1986b. The dual approach to the value of information: an appraisal of use and exchange values. Information Processing and Management, 22(5), 373–383.

———— 1987. Economics of information. Annual Review of Information Science and Technology, 22, 3–35.

Roberts, S.A., ed. 1984. Costing and the economics of library and information services. Aslib, London, UK.

Robinson, S. 1986. Analyzing the information economy: tools and techniques. Information Processing and Management, 22(3), 183–202.

Roderer, N.J.; King, D.W.; Brouard, S.E. 1983. The use and value of defense technical information center products and services. Defense Technical Information Center, Alexandria, VA, USA.

Rondinelli, D.A. 1983. Development projects as policy experiments, an adaptive approach to development administration. Methuen, London, UK.

Ruben, B.D. 1992. The communication–information relationship in system-theoric perspective. Journal of the American Society for Information Science, 43(1), 15–27.

Salinas Bascur, R. 1986. Forget the NWICO and begin all over again: a report of the collaborative project on information overload and information underuse. Global Learning Division, United Nations University, Tokyo, Japan.

Salmona, J. 1981. La contribution de l'information socio-économique au développement : esquisse d'une analyse critique et propositions. Association Internationale Données pour le Développement, Marseille, France.

Salome, B.; Charmes, J. 1988. In-service training: five Asian experiences. Organisation for Economic Co-operation and Development, Paris, France.

Samarajiva, R. 1989. IDRC information science projects and priorities in Sri Lanka: a countrywide assessment. Information Sciences and Systems Division, International Development Research Centre, Ottawa, ON, Canada.

Samarajiva, R.; Shields, P. 1990. Value issues in telecommunication resource allocation in the Third World. In Lundstedt, S.B., ed., Telecommunications, values and the public interest. Ablex, Norwood, NJ, USA. pp. 227–253.

Sangway, D. 1989. Government approach to information management. Aslib Proceedings, 41(5), 179–187.

Saracevic, T. 1980. Perception of the needs for scientific and technical information in less developed countries. Journal of Documentation, 36 (3), 214—267.

Saracevic, T.; Kantor, P.; Chamis, A.Y.; Trivison, D. 1988. A study of information seeking and retrieving. Journal of the American Society for Information Science, 39(3), 161–216.

Scandizzo, P.L.; Knundsen, O.K. 1980. The evaluation of the benefits of basic needs policy. American Journal of Agricultural Economics, 62(1), 46–57.

Schwüchow, W. 1977. The economic analysis and evaluation of information and documentation systems. Information Processing and Management, 13(5), 267–272.

Shapiro, F.R. 1992. Origins of bibliometrics, citation indexing and citation analysis: the neglected legal literature. Journal of the American Society for Information Science, 43(5), 337–339.

Siegel, E.R. 1982. Transfer of information to health practitioners. In Dervin, B., Voight, M.J., ed., Progress in communication sciences, vol. 3. Ablex Publishing, Norwood, NJ, USA. pp. 311–334.

Slamecka, V. 1982. The inclination toward information use. In Sweeney, G.P., ed., Information and the transformation of society. Elsevier, Amsterdam, Netherlands.

Slater, M. 1988. Social scientists' needs in the 1980s. Journal of Documentation, 44(3), 226–237.

Squire, L.; van der Tak, H.G. 1975. Economic analysis of projects. Johns Hopkins University Press, Baltimore, MD, USA. World Bank Research Publications.

Srivanasan, T.N. 1977. Poverty: some measurement problems. In Proceedings of the 41st session of the International Statistical Institute. International Statistical Institute, New Delhi, India. pp. 1–16.

Stone, M.B. 1992. Documentation for development: a view from the North. In Strengthening cooperation in documentation for development. A seminar on networking with special emphasis on NGOs, 3–6 September 1991, Paris, France. Chr. Michelsen Institute, Fantoft, Bergen, Norway. pp. 35–49.

Stonier, T. 1983. The wealth of information: a profile of the post-industrial economy. Thames, Methuen, London, UK.

———— 1991. Towards a new theory of information. Journal of Information Science, 17(5), 257–263.

Strassmann, P.A. 1976. Managing the costs of information. Harvard Business Review, September/October, 133–142.

———— 1985. Information payoff: the transformation of work in the electronic age. The Free Press, New York, NY, USA.

_____ 1990. The business value of computers. Information Economics Press, New Canaan, CN, USA.

Stroetmann, K.A. 1991. Die vernetze Weltgemeinschaft: Potentiale und Risken. 17. Internationalen Kolloquium für Information und Dokumentation in Verbindung mit 2. Internationales Symposium für Informationswissenschaft, 4–7 November 1991, Oberhof.

Sturges, P.; Mchombu, K.; Neill, R. 1991. Indigenous knowledge base in African development. Social Intelligence, 1(3), 213–237.

Taylor, R.S. 1982. Value-added processes in the information life cycle. Journal of the American Society for Information Science, 33, 341–346.

_____ 1986. Value-added processes in information systems. Ablex Publishing, Norwood, NJ, USA.

_____ 1991. Information use environments. In Dervin, B., Voight, M.J., ed., Progress in communication sciences, vol. 10. Ablex Publishing, Norwood, NJ, USA. pp. 217–255.

Trilateral Group. 1988. Glenerin declaration. FID News Bulletin, 38(5), 37–38.

Tiamiyu, M.A. 1992. The relationships between source use and work complexity, decision-maker discretion and activity duration in Nigerian government ministries. International Journal of Information Management, 12(2), 130–141.

Turnbaum, D.; Salome, B.; Schwarz, A., ed. 1990. The informal sector revisited. Organisation for Economic Co-operation and Development, Paris, France.

UNDP (United Nations Development Programme). 1992. World report on human development 1992. Oxford University Press, New York, NY, USA.

UNIDO (United Nations Industrial Development Organization). 1978. Guide to practical project appraisal, social benefit–cost analysis in developing countries. UNIDO, Vienna, Austria.

Urquhardt, B.; Childers, E. 1991. Towards a more effective United Nations. Development Dialogue, 1(2), 1–40.

Van House, N.A. 1984. Research on the economics of libraries. Library Trends, 32(4), 407–423.

Varlejs, J., ed. 1982. The economics of information. McFarland, London, UK.

Veenhaven, R. 1987. Cultural bias in ratings of perceived life quality. Social Indicators Research, 19, 329–334.

Vickers, P.H. 1978. A cost analysis approach to national information. United Nations Educational, Scientific and Cultural Organisation, Paris, France. PGI/78/WS/3.

Vitro, R.A. 1990. Information: a strategy for economic growth. Presented at the state-of-the-art institute, 6–8 November 1989, Washington, DC. Special Libraries Association, Washington, DC, USA. pp. 87–100.

Vogel, J. 1991. The intellectual property of natural and artificial information. CIRCIT Newsletter (Melbourne, Australia), 3(5), 7.

Walker, P. 1989. Famine early warning systems: victims and destitution. Earthscan, London, UK.

Weil, B. 1980. Benefits from research use of the published literature at the Exxon Research Center. In Jackson, E.B., ed., Special librarianship: a new reader. Scarecrow Press, NJ, USA. pp. 586–594.

Wilson, S.R.; Starr-Schneidkraut, N.; Cooper, M.D. 1989. Use of the critical incident technique to evaluate the impact of MEDLINE. American Institute for Research in the Behavioral Sciences, Palo Alto, CA, USA.

Wilson, T.D. 1981. On user studies and information needs. Journal of Documentation, 37(1), 3–15.

Yovits, M.C.; Foulk, C.R. 1985. Experiments and analysis of information use and value in a decision-making context. Journal of the American Society of Information Science, 36(2), 63–81.

Zachert, M.J.; Williams, R.V. 1986. Marketing measures for information services. Special Libraries, 77(2), 61–70.

Zeisel, J. 1981. Inquiry by design: tools for environment-behaviour research. Cambridge University Press, Cambridge MA, USA.

Selected documents on computer conferencing

Balson, D.A., ed. 1985. International computer-based conference on biotechnology: a case study. International Development Research Centre, Ottawa, ON, Canada. IDRC-241e.

Dobrov, G.M.; Randolph, R.H.; Rauch, W.D. 1979. New options for team research via international computer networks. Scientometrics, 1(5/6), 387–404.

Harasim, L.; Johnson, E.M. 1985. Computer conferencing and online education: designing for the medium. Canadian Journal of Information Science, 10, 1–15.

Hiltz, S.R. 1978. The computer conference. Journal of Communication, 28(3), 157–163.

Hiltz, S.R.; Turoff, M. 1978. The network nation. Addison-Wesley, Reading, MA, USA.

Parker, L.A.; Olgren, C.H., ed. 1984. The teleconferencing resources book: a guide to application and planning. Elsevier, Amsterdam, Netherlands.

Perrin, P.; Gensollen, M., ed. 1992. La communication plurielle : l'interaction dans les téléconférences. La Documentation Française, Paris, France. Collection technique et scientifique des télécommunications.

Rosenbaum, H.; Snyder, H. 1991. An investigation of emerging norms in computer mediated conferences: an empirical study of computer conferencing. In Proceedings of the 54th annual meeting of the American Society for Information Science, vol. 28. Learned Information, Medford, NJ, USA. pp. 15–23.

Steinfield, C.W. 1986. Computer mediated communication systems. Annual Review of Information Science and Technology, 21, 167–202.

Unpublished documents produced by the project

Griffiths, J.M., rapporteur. 1993. Post-computer conference workshop on assessment indicators for the impact of information on development, 1–3 March 1993, Nairobi, Kenya: report of Working Group 2. IDRC, Ottawa, ON, Canada. 8 pp.

Griffiths, J.M.; Horton, F.W., rapporteurs. 1993. Post-computer conference workshop on assessment indicators for the impact of information on development, 1–3 March 1993, Nairobi, Kenya: integrated report of Working Groups 1 and 2. IDRC, Ottawa, ON, Canada. 24 pp.

Horton, F.W., Jr, rapporteur. 1993. Post-computer conference workshop on assessment indicators for the impact of information on development, 1–3 March 1993, Nairobi, Kenya: report of Working Group 1. IDRC, Ottawa, ON, Canada. 16 pp.

IDRC (International Development Research Centre). 1992. Assessment indicators for the impact of information on development: problem statement. IDRC, Ottawa, ON, Canada. 1 p.

_____ 1992. Assessment indicators for the impact of information on development: complete record of all contributions to the computer conference 4 April to 8 August 1992. IDRC, Ottawa, ON, Canada. 147 pp. (restricted distribution)

_____ 1992. Assessment indicators for the impact of information on development: complete record of all contributions to the computer conference 8 August to 8 November 1992. IDRC, Ottawa, ON, Canada. 95 pp. (restricted distribution)

Menou, M.J. 1992. Assessment indicators for the impact of information on development: an initial investigation through a computer conference: preliminary outline. IDRC, Ottawa, ON, Canada. 11 pp.

_____ compiler. 1992. Assessment indicators for the impact of information on development: summary of transactions 6 April to 6 July 1992. IDRC, Ottawa, ON, Canada. 14 pp.

_____ compiler. 1992. Assessment indicators for the impact of information on development: summary of transactions 7 July to 9 September 1992. IDRC, Ottawa, ON, Canada. 17 pp.

_____ compiler. 1992. Assessment indicators for the impact of information on development: summary of transactions 10 September to 6 October 1992. IDRC, Ottawa, ON, Canada. 1 p.

_____ compiler. 1992. Assessment indicators for the impact of information on development: summary of transactions 7 October to 20 November 1992. IDRC, Ottawa, ON, Canada. 7 pp.

_____ compiler. 1993. Assessment indicators for the impact of information on development: preliminary report of an international computer conference. IDRC, Ottawa, ON, Canada. 93 pp. (restricted distribution)

Thorngate, W. 1993. Evaluation of an international computer conference on assessment indicators for the impact of information on development. Carleton University and IDRC, Ottawa, ON, Canada. 20 pp. (restricted distribution, in preparation for publication)

Index

——————■——————

Access to information   31, 46–48, 76
    equality of access   46–47
Assessment framework (*see* Impact assessment framework)
Assessment indicators (*see* Indicators)
Assessment methods (*see* Impact assessment)

Benefit assessment (*see* Impact assessment)
Benefit indicators (*see* Indicators)
Benefits
    concepts   15–19
    and costs   21, 49–59
    and development goals   38
    direct   44
    indirect   44
    and information needs   54–57
    and information users   39, 47
    local level   37–39
    long-term   45, 53
    political aspects   48–49
    for organizations   59–61, 72–73
    in rural communities   129–134
    short-term   44–45, 53, 60
    types   44–46

CARICOM Project   103, 105
    benefits   158–160
    impact assessment   141–160
    indicators   158–160

CARICOM Project *(cont'd)*
    management 146
    methodology 146–155
    objectives 143–144
    outputs 145
    overview 141–143
    project evaluation 155–156
    users 146, 159
Common Pool Resources (CPR) Model 57–59
Communication 100–103
    cycle 66–68, 70
    tradition and 28, 39–40
Computer conference
    consultative panel 4–5, 11–13, 115–119
    documents 12
    effectiveness 13–14
    evaluation 13–14, 112–114
    messages 11–13
    need for 3
    objectives 1–2
    participants 3–6, 10–14, 81–82, 115–119
    proceedings 5, 11–13
    schedule 6, 10–11
    summaries 13
    topics 6–11
Computer conferencing *(see* Computer conference)
Conferencing messages *(see* Computer conference, messages)
Constituencies *(see* Information use environments)
Coping information 54–56
Correlation analysis 65
Cost–benefit analysis (CBA) 21, 49–61, 107
    assumptions 51–52
    steps 49–50, 121–127
CoSy Computer Conferencing System 3, 10
Culture
    and information 26–29, 39–40

Decision-making
    and information 27, 34, 48–54
Development
    causes 20

Development *(cont'd)*
 definition 16, 22–23
 indicators 22–23
Direct benefits *(see* Benefits, direct)

Edifying information 54–57
Electronic networks 46–47
Endogenous information 23, 25–26, 28–29
Enlightening information 54–56
Enriching information 54–57
Environment *(see* Information use environments)
Exogenous information 25

Formal information 26–29

Helping information 54–56

IDRC *(see* International Development Research Centre)
Impact assessment
 anecdotes 76–78
 case studies 129–139
 criteria 34, 75–76, 135–139
 dissemination 105
 field tests 105, 107–108
 information projects 69–79
 information use environments 66–69, 73–78
 international cooperation 109–111
 market studies 78–79
 monitoring and evaluation 108–109
 organizations 72–73
 prerequisites 91–93
 research needs 111–112
 training 106–107
Impact assessment framework 89–103, 107
 CARICOM project 141–160
 evaluation 113
 input–output categories 97–100
 input–output matrix 101–103
 model 93–97
 structure 93–97

Indicators 33–35, 61, 70–72, 84–103, 158–160
    characteristics 63–66
    framework 84–86
    functions 91
    long-term 125
    mid-term 124
    and organizations 72–73
    purposes 64
    short-term 124
    types 64, 97
    users 19
Indirect benefits (*see* Benefits, indirect)
Informal information 26–27
Information
    benefits (*see* Benefits)
    categories 25–26
    centres (*see* Resource centres)
    costs (*see* Cost–benefit analysis)
    definition 23
    development 32
    impact 15–21, 26, 33–35, 69–72
    infrastructure 30–31
    nature of 89–90
    needs hierarchy 54–57
    policies 30, 55–57
    role 24–25, 90
    services 30–32, 42
    society 23, 26
    sociocultural influences 27–29
    specialists 4–6, 12, 28
    systems 30–31, 105–106, 111
    users 17–19, 27–29, 31–32, 43, 47–48
    value 24–25, 47–48, 90
Information Resources Management (IRM) 40–42
Information Use Environment (IUE) Model 67–69
Information use environments 18, 66–70
    anecdotes 76–78
    field testing 107–108
    impact assessment 73–78
    monitoring and evaluation 108–109

Input–output
    categories 97–100
    matrix 101–103
International cooperation
    in information research 109–111
International Development Research Centre (IDRC) 3–6, 10, 23
    Library 12
    projects 82–83, 105–107

Knowledge
    definition 23
    local level 25
    society 23
Knowledge Worker Productivity Model 59–60, 70

Long-term benefits (*see* Benefits, long-term)

Market studies
    in impact assessment 78–79
    of information needs in organizations 70–71
Messages (*see* Computer conference, messages)
Models 18, 34, 54–61, 67–70, 86, 93–97

North–South cooperation
    in information activities 29

Oral tradition 39–40
Organization Resource Management (ORM) Model 59–61
Organizations
    benefits of information 59–61, 72–73
    information management 41–42
    information needs 70–71

Parameters (*see* Indicators)
Post-conference workshop
    evaluation 113
    objectives 81
    participants 81–82, 115–119
    schedule 82–84
    working groups 82–87, 113
Production factors 16–17, 59

Raw information 6, 29
Regression analysis 65
Research needs 111–112
Resource centres
    in rural communities 129–134

Short-term benefits (*see* Benefits, short-term)
Social intelligence 24
Specialists (*see* Information, specialists)
Surveys 65
Sustainability
    of information systems 111

Trilateral Group 33–34

Visual tradition 40

Wisdom
    definition 23–24
Working groups
    evaluation 113
    guidelines 83
    proceedings 84–87

About the Institution

The International Development Research Centre (IDRC) is a public corporation created by the Parliament of Canada in 1970 to support technical and policy research to help meet the needs of developing countries. The Centre is active in the fields of environment and natural resources, social sciences, health sciences, and information sciences and systems. Regional offices are located in Africa, Asia, Latin America, and the Middle East.

About the Publisher

IDRC Books publishes research results and scholarly studies on global and regional issues related to sustainable and equitable development. As a specialist in development literature, *IDRC Books* contributes to the body of knowledge on these issues to further the cause of global understanding and equity. IDRC publications are sold through its head office in Ottawa, Canada, as well as by IDRC's agents and distributors around the world.